The Windsor

Courts-martial of 1854:

Drunkenness, Gambling, Whoring and Bullying in the Victorian Army

The Windsor Courts-martial of 1854:

Drunkenness, Gambling, Whoring and Bullying in the Victorian Army

The extraordinary events of 1854 at Windsor transcribed, annotated and edited by

Major Colin Robins

Withycut House 2015

First published 2015
Withycut House
12 Enville Road
Bowdon
Cheshire WA14 2PQ
United Kingdom

ISBN 978-1-899-244-05-8

Typeset in Times New Roman
By the publisher
Printed and bound in Great Britain by
CPI Group(UK)Ltd, Croydon, CR0 4YY

To all members of the armed forces of the Crown
who have experienced injustice in any form

Contents

An Index would be impracticable as the officers of the regiment are mentioned repeatedly and their full details are in Hart's Army List at Appendix G.. Illustrations form the centre pages. The engraving of Perry's court-martial is by courtesy of the Council of the National Army Museum, London. The uniform of the Line Infantry and the cartoon from Punch are from the Author's collection

Introduction and Acknowledgements

My military history speciality is study of the Crimean War and for some ten years I was privileged to edit the journal of the Crimean War Research Society, aptly named 'The War Correspondent' as it was that war in which William Howard Russell, generally accepted as the first of that noble breed, came to fame with his regular and often excoriating reports for The Times.

Interest in the 46th (South Devon) Foot was aroused when, on behalf of the trustees, Major Hugo White, DL, the Curator of the Regimental Museum of the Duke of Cornwall's Light Infantry, at Bodmin Castle in Cornwall, allowed me to see, and then transcribe for publication, the journal of Lieutenant Richard Llewellyn (sometimes rendered as Lluellyn). Llewellyn was outraged at the dreadful treatment of his regiment which arrived in the Crimea just after the Battle of Inkerman and was immediately faced with repeated duty in the trenches in the dreadful weather then being experienced. The number of casualties from illness soared and as the fewer and fewer men left available for duty fell, so the duty came round more and more often. The inevitable result is obvious, and the regiment was effectively destroyed. Llewellyn was certain that this was no suicide, but murder and there could be no other title for his journal but 'The Murder of a Regiment'.

Major White also kindly allowed me to see, and in due course publish, the diary of Captain Nicholas

Dunscombe, of the same regiment and that became 'Captain Dunscombe's Diary – the Real Crimean War'. Study of the 46th revealed the unusual circumstance that only one company travelled to the Crimea with the main body of the British army, the 'Army of the East', and the rest of the regiment, including Llewellyn, arrived late. Probing revealed that the main body had been delayed as it had been necessary to detain them in England while one, later two, officers were court-martialled. Major White was a little reticent about this. He himself had served in the 13th, Prince Albert's Regiment of Light Infantry, and only successive amalgamations had brought the 46th (and the 32[nd)]) into the same regiment. One does not relish washing linen in public even if it is not strictly one's own.

As well as Major White who sparked my initial interest, several others have given huge help in the preparation of this work as it was necessary to find and examine many sources. Bert Gedin, Doctor Mike Hinton, the late Major Bill Billett (in Australia), all helped, and above all, thanks are due to Michael Hargreave Mawson, doyen of historians of the 46th, whose encouragement and active assistance have been of the utmost importance.

Investigation of the circumstances astonished and appalled the present writer, a retired officer, and he will be surprised if readers do not feel the same anger.

Colin Robins
Bowdon, 2015

Prologue

In 1853 and the early part of 1854, Great Britain slid inexorably towards a war with Russia, and a British expeditionary force, or 'Army of the East' as it was known, together with one from our French Allies, was slowly assembled and moved out to Turkey via Malta. First the British and French began to dig hasty defensive works at Bulair, north of Gallipoli, for the Russians had crossed the River Pruth and invaded Moldavia and Wallachia, provinces of the Ottoman Empire. It was feared they would soon be in Constantinople: Gallipoli would then be a secure rear base from which captured Turkey could be liberated. However, as the news from modern Bulgaria improved, the British moved north to Scutari, across the Bosphorus opposite the Turkish capital. Later they moved on to camp near Varna, on the Black Sea in modern Bulgaria but then part of the Ottoman Empire, some one hundred and fifty miles north of Constantinople, ready to oppose the Russian invaders. As it did so, one regiment - the 46th (South Devonshire) Foot - was represented by only two companies. The regiment's headquarters and the remaining rifle companies were missing from the scene of war. They were, in fact, still at the regiment's base, the Infantry Barracks at Windsor.

They were there still as the Russians retreated across the River Danube to their own territory, and Lord Raglan, the aged British Commander-in-Chief, and the ailing French Marshal St Arnaud, agonised over what to do next. The invader had been repelled, and the Allies' objective had thus been achieved, but under the pressure of public opinion the British government realised that the huge army which they had assembled and transported so far with such difficulty, and at such expense, would now have to do something decisive to punish the Russian agressor for his actions. In a badly drafted, vague and uncertain despatch, the Cabinet had instructed Raglan to take Sevastopol and destroy it as a naval base - but only if he thought this wise, and otherwise to act as he saw fit. But the unwritten meaning was clear. The public demanded action, and the government expected their Commander-in-Chief, whatever the difficulties, to provide it. Raglan, who had always tried to act as his former mentor, the Duke of Wellington, would have done, consulted Sir George Brown, one of his divisional commanders who was also a Peninsular veteran. Sir George stated that the Duke would never have contemplated an invasion without knowledge of the enemy's strength and dispositions: there was no information on how many men Russia had in the Crimea, let alone where they were. But Sir George also pointed out that the home government was clearly keen for Sevastopol to be captured, and if Raglan did not do it, then they would undoubtedly find a commander who would. On that uncertain foundation, the plan to invade the Crimea went ahead. Sir George was sent to Constantinople to organize the purchase of small boats which could land troops, and reconnaissances of the Crimean west coast took place. Eventually the invasion fleet, British, French and Turkish, set sail before a final decision had been made as to where it should land and, while it was actually afloat, the beach at Old Fort, some 30 miles north of Sevastopol, was chosen.

The landing duly took place on 14th September 1854 and over the subsequent few days, for the disembarkation of cavalry and artillery horses was a difficult operation, aggravated as the weather deteriorated after the first day, and took some time. Several more days were spent in re-organising, and then the march towards Sevastopol began. On 20th September the Allies reached a natural defensive position on the River Alma, where the Russian commander had promised he could hold up the enemy for three weeks. Some three hours of bloody fighting, largely by the British who were placed opposite and in front of the enemy's strongest redoubts and heaviest guns, led to heavy casualties but in three hours the position was won and the Russian army fled in confusion, scattering equipment and stores as they ran. The victory was not however exploited and again precious days were spent burying the dead, tending the wounded, sorting out stores and regrouping. Then the march resumed, skirted the town of Sevastopol (at that time scarcely defended), and after token resistance the little town and harbour of Balaklava fell to the British. It was selected as the port to supply the force. The French based themselves on the Bay of Kamiesch some ten miles to the west, nearer Sevastopol, and not vulnerable to frontal assault from the Russians, as Balaklava was. More time was now spent in landing siege artillery, specially shipped from England, and heavy guns from the fleet, with sailors to man the latter. Formal siege works were prepared: the first trenches or 'parallels', out of range of the enemy guns, were dug and batteries for the guns were constructed. On 17th October the First Bombardment was opened simultaneously from the land batteries, and the combined British and French fleets (which did little damage, but suffered a great deal themselves). The Allied infantry stood by ready to assault the town to exploit the success of the bombardment, which was confidently expected, but early on the first day the French suffered a serious blow when one of their principal magazines was blown up, and their firing was suspended. The moment for a successful infantry assault passed. It was a long time before it occurred again.

Surprisingly, Sevastopol was never truly besieged, for a strip of land beside the river and sea was held by them and formed a northern 'corridor' through which they passed troops and stores, in and out of the town, throughout the next months. A few days after the unsuccessful bombardment, on 25th October, a large part of the Russian army, which was not in the town but roaming the country behind the British force, made a determined attempt to seize the harbour of Balaklava and thus to cut the British from their supply base. Seizing a line of four forts which formed an outer defence of the harbour and which were held by Turkish troops with two or three borrowed British guns in each, the Russians turned towards the harbour led by their cavalry. The famous incident described by Russell of *The Times* as the 'thin red streak topped with a line of steel', which later came to be known as the 'thin red line', and the Charge of the Heavy Cavalry Brigade under Sir James

Scarlett followed. The Russian threat to the harbour of Balaklava was repulsed, but then followed the infamous incident of the mistaken order and the English Light Cavalry Brigade was all but destroyed as an effective force by a brave but completely pointless charge in the north valley. The outer ring of forts, and control of the only metalled road which covered part of the route from Balaklava to the British camp, was lost as inertia gripped the British Commander-in-Chief and the two infantry divisional commanders who had been ordered down to the plain with their divisions to recover the redoubts. Worse, the harbour, which had been crammed with merchant ships loaded with stores for the army, was evacuated in near-panic as the news that the Russians were bearing down towards it reached the sailors there. This left the ships outside the harbour in the open sea and particularly vulnerable to the storm which was to follow on 14th November with enormous loss of life, shipping and precious stores. Although overlooked by many commentators, this was probably the worst effect of the failure to regain the lost redoubts.

The following day, 26th October, the Russians made a sortie from the town and again attacked the English position in some strength but were beaten off in an engagement usually known as 'Little Inkerman', to distinguish it from the true Battle of Inkerman, which followed on 5th November. In the latter, some 40,000 Russian troops, with 97, mostly heavy, guns, managed to seize the high ground of Inkerman heights, left undefended by Raglan who was using every available man to prepare trenches from which an assault of

Sevastopol could be made. The battle which followed lasted nearly ten hours and was one of the most hard-fought and bloody battles the British army has ever fought.

All this time two companies of the 46th Foot, which had left England on 22 July 1854 with the main British army, formed part of 4th Division, and indeed they particularly distinguished themselves at Inkerman where they formed part of the contingent led until his death by the divisional commander Sir George Cathcart (who may have been trying to atone, by foolhardy bravery, for his inaction at Balaklava). But the main body, the regimental headquarters and remaining six rifle companies were absent and they did not arrive in the Crimea until after all the well-known staged battles.

The reason for this was a Victorian *scandale célèbre*. A General Court-martial was in progress at Windsor to hear allegations that one of the regiment's officers had violently attacked a brother officer. The Commanding Officer, Senior Major, Adjutant, and many of the regiment's other officers were required in England for the proceedings as officials or witnesses, and despite the army's desperate need for as many units as could be found, only two companies could be manned by officers who, it was decided, would not be needed for the trial, and only those two companies had therefore been able to sail.

The story which unfolded before the court in August 1854 was published at length in the newspapers, including *The Times*, and attracted widespread attention throughout England, not just from the upper classes, but also from the new, newspaper-reading, middle class, ever vigilant for examples of injustice, especially if it seemed that the middle class was being oppressed by its betters. Perhaps not since the scandal a few years earlier involving Lord Brudenell, (who as Lord Cardigan led the Light Cavalry Brigade in the famous charge at Balaklava referred to earlier, but at that time commanding the 15th Hussars), had there been such public interest in embarrassing happenings in a regimental officers' mess, and much corresponding irritation in the military establishment, serving and retired, at what was seen as impertinent interference in private army affairs by newspapers and the general public.

However, as a picture of drunkenness, gambling, whoring and bullying in the 46th officers' mess slowly emerged, the one court-martial became, in due course, three — and the main body of the regiment was delayed so much that in the end it did not arrive in the Crimea until 7 November, having missed the main army's landing, the Battles of the Alma, Balaklava and the desperate struggle of Inkerman as well. The events at Windsor in 1854, followed by the Courts-Martial, had disgraced the regiment and had actually made it late for the war.

Chapter 1 - The army in 1850

The composition and organization of the British army in 1850 was not very different from that which had fought in the Peninsula and at Waterloo. (Nor, in fact, had the uniforms and equipment changed much, but that is another story, outside the scope of this work.)

'Other Ranks', that is private soldiers, were still largely, in the Duke of Wellington's famous words, 'the scum of the earth'. He considered new recruits the most drunken and worst specimens of humanity. In ninety-nine cases out of a hundred they enlisted on account of some idle, irregular or even vicious motive. Only iron discipline could control their anti-social habits and tendencies[1]. It is important to realize that these remarks were not made by him from contempt, nor even of complaint. They represented the position as it was - and it has been suggested[2] that it is how Wellington thought it

---

[1] As recorded in the Duke's published despatches and correspondence, and quoted by Dr. E.M. Spiers in his thorough *The Army and Society, 1815-1914.*
[2] See the description of 'the British army in 1850' in Colonel H Moyse-Bartlett's excellent paper with that title in the *Journal of the Society for Army Historical Research,* Vol 52, pp 221 to 237. No study of the army at that time can overlook this authoritative paper.

ought to be. He did not think it right to impose the hard, brutish life of a soldier on the more useful members of society. Let those who could do nothing else be soldiers: society's misfits, criminals and paupers (of which there was a steady supply). This group was incapable of making a contribution to normal civilian society, but when rigorously disciplined and courageously led, was able to show courage and endurance unequalled in Europe.

This idea that the services should recruit from the 'dregs and refuse' of the population was certainly current at the turn of the century, and a writer has quoted[3] an anonymous contributor to the *Edinburgh Review* in 1801 who thought the process socially beneficial, for all countries contain a proportion of these indigent creatures, criminals and men of bad character, and in the services they were kept within bounds of behaviour by the strict discipline, while they were of course separated from the healthier branches of society. Thus at the same time the army relieved the community of the problem of such persons, but made them useful to their country. It was the only welfare service provided by the state.

Wellington's positive attitude to improvements in the common soldiers' conditions, which inevitably would make their lives less brutish and thus tend to attract recruits of better character, does question whether he really did hold this somewhat pessimistic view. True, he seems to have favoured the retention of flogging, as a last resort, and it is well-documented that in the last year or two of his life, his discharge of the duties of Commander-in-Chief was but nominal.

---

[3]CC Bayley in his *Mercenaries for the Crimea,* pub Montreal 1977, which contains an excellent study of the British Army's recruiting before the Crimean War, as well as its attempts to solve the problem by finding mercenaries.

His daily attendance at Horse Guards, riding to and fro from Apsley House ('Number 1, London'), but spending most of each day sleeping in his office, was of little effect. He had even been obliged to implement Parliament's demands for economy by abolishing the Royal Waggon Train which he himself had found essential in his campaigning against Napoleon. But he had not resisted all changes and, for example, his rather grudging approval of the new Minié rifle[4] gave the infantry a personal weapon which probably did more than any other single thing to save the British from defeat in the early stages of the Crimean War. He had also accepted the introduction of amenities for the common soldier such as schools (1849) and several others (see below). A biographer has written[5] that it was the intensity of his obsession with the country's defencelessness during his last ten years (1842-1852) that forbade him to risk inventions and new ideas *where old, tried methods were available* (my emphasis). This is a very long way from opposing all change, as has been alleged by some. So, although most writers[6] have recorded his resolute

---

[4] He insisted, however, that the new weapon, properly referred to as the Pattern '51 but commonly called after Captain Minié who invented its rifling system, should have the same calibre as the Pattern '44 musket it was to replace, overlooking that this meant that the 'bullet', now shaped with a point, was consequently much heavier than the ball it replaced, reducing the number of rounds the soldier could be expected to carry. He also ordered that the new weapon be referred to as a 'rifle musket' and was adamant that the men should not be allowed to 'dress in green' as the existing rifle regiments did.

[5] Elizabeth Longford in her scholarly but entertaining book *Wellington, Pillar of State,* pub London 1972.

[6] For example, Hew Strachan in his excellent essay 'The early Victorian army and the nineteenth-century revolution in government', *The English Historical Review,* vol 95 (1980).

opposition to many changes, especially those in organisation and administration, his terms of office as Master General of the Ordnance, and (twice) as Commander-in-Chief, did not prevent considerable changes for the better in the soldier's daily life. Some improvements were also introduced in the gaps between his periods in office, and others which he had opposed were quickly brought in when he had left office on his death.

However, even as conditions did therefore, slowly, improve during the second quarter of the Nineteenth Century the army continued to be recruited from the very poorest and most ignorant section of society. After Waterloo, its size was steadily and drastically reduced until the strength was little more than half its 'Napoleonic' maximum. The number of recruits sought annually fell sharply too, but by the 1820s had stabilized so that around 6,000 were needed each year. Civil unrest in the 1830s led Parliament to agree higher estimates to try and recruit 12,000 and by 1842 army strength had risen to 95,000. The canal and railway booms, and the large number of labourers they needed, and the rising tide of emigration in both Ireland and in England, had provided serious competition for the available supply of unemployed in town and country, but especially difficult economic conditions in the British Isles during the 'Hungry Forties' produced over 24,000 recruits in 1846 as the Irish potato famine reached its worst point. Almost two-thirds were agricultural labourers, less than a third were industrial workers and under a twentieth were clerks and shop assistants. A handful were sons of gentlemen or professional men in reduced circumstances. Most of these were of course unemployed when they enlisted, and few had had any education at all. A disproportionately high number of soldiers had always been recruited from the Irish and, to a lesser extent, Scottish populations. Most of the Irish were from rural backgrounds, but the Scots were increasingly urban. After the 1846 famine the number of Irish recruits fell steadily as young men who might otherwise have enlisted emigrated instead to the United States, and the whole army became less and less recruited from the agricultural labourers who were regarded as ideal soldiers: much stronger and fitter than their urban contemporaries, and also more malleable, obedient and contented with their lot[7] .

England had never looked kindly on the concept of a standing army and fears of militarism were perhaps most prominent in the Nineteenth Century, and not just among radical politicians and writers. But there were even more controversial political matters to arouse the populace, and the army was too small and too widely scattered for opposition to it to be sustained. However all parties agreed that every possible economy should be made and expenditure on the army was steadily cut. The nation particularly resented the cost of recruiting. The cheapest labour obtained at lowest cost had always been the object. For years, the term of service had been for life, or until the Crown at its discretion (and when it suited its convenience) discharged the man. Volunteers found it easy to enter, but hard to escape. Conscription had been authorized from time to time in the 18th Century in time of war, but was finally abandoned in 1780 and not reintroduced until the First World War. The army favoured long service which saved the expense of attracting and training new recruits, and the loss of trained and experienced men in their prime. In any case, with regiments spending long periods overseas it was not easy to release men after a fixed term. Nevertheless, during the Napoleonic Wars limited enlistment had been introduced by Parliament, though the recruit was allowed to opt for life if he wished. In 1829 the Adjutant General forbad further short enlistments so that life became the only choice, but in 1847, largely in the hope of

---

[7] Quoted from a Parliamentary Commission by Spiers, *op cit.*

stimulating volunteers, Parliament again intervened with legislation, and the Limited Enlistment Act made the only engagement for the infantry one of an initial ten years, with possible re-enlistment for another eleven, making twenty-one years in all - quickly dubbed by the soldiers 'pontoon'[8]. The cavalryman's first term was for twelve years and the same term applied for artillerymen and sappers, with voluntary re-enlistment for another twelve. On foreign service a soldier could be held for a further two years beyond his agreed term if judged necessary by his commanding officer. Thus in 1850 the army consisted of soldiers who had been recruited under three separate systems, but most of them had enlisted for life. The feeling that it was a disgrace for a family if a son 'went for a soldier' persisted and his family often mourned as if he had died. In fact their loss was similar for they might never see him again: a posting to the West Indies or another part of the world where disease was rife might well result in death - for many it did[9].

For those on lifetime engagements who had retained their health, there were only two ways of escape. Provided he had served for at least ten years, a man could buy his release for fifteen pounds - then of course an appreciable sum. If he had served fifteen years he might, if the army did not need him, be discharged for nothing. The only other way out was to desert - a most serious offence punishable under the Mutiny Act by 'death, penal servitude or such other punishment as a court-martial shall award.' Desertion was

---

[8] The card game in which the object is to achieve a hand totalling twenty-one points.

[9] The death rate in the Windward, Leeward Islands and Jamaica from 1800 to 1850 peaked in some years at over 300 per thousand, most from tropical fevers. Philip D. Curtin, *Death by Migration,* Cambridge University Press, 1989.

automatically assumed after twenty-one days absence without leave, a concept familiar to those who have served much more recently. Nor was death just an unused threat: it was sometimes awarded, and lesser punishments were accompanied by branding, but seldom by discharge of the culprit lest it should come to be seen as a way out.

Recruiting was still done by roving recruiting teams, each under a recruiting sergeant who, often by first plying them with drink, would lure simple country lads into accepting the King's (or Queen's) shilling. A recruiting sergeant writing just before 1850, quoted by Bayley[10], thought that over half of the recruits were unemployed; of the rest, some 20 percent were idle and thought a soldier's life would be easy. 10 percent were postively of bad character, and the same percentage were seeking a life of adventure. The rest were of various classes, and included some criminals hoping to escape punishment. Another recruiting sergeant writing at about the same time[11] admitted that he went to the very places where he was least likely to meet respectable men. At the public house, and similar disreputable places, he would find the idle and dissolute, most of whom were confirmed drunkards. The potential recruit would be flattered, given a completely false picture of glamorous life as a soldier, and would be tempted by talk of the bounty money which would be paid to him on enlistment. He was not told that he would have to buy his kit from that bounty money and that the cost of the kit was greater than the bounty so that he would inevitably start his army life in debt![12] This

---

[10]CC Bayley, *op cit.*

[11]*Ibid*

[12]Layard, a reforming MP, had pointed out in the House of Commons in the 1840s that in the infantry the bounty was £3.17.6d and the stoppages for kit were £4.9.10½d. The short- fall for the cavalryman was even larger. Quoted by CC Bayley, *op cit.*

was one of the greatest grievances which often led to desertion, most common in the first year of service. More recruits were lost when they, or their families, raised and paid the so-called 'smart money' which bought the recruit's discharge. Within four days of enlistment the recruit had to be brought before a magistrate to attest that he had not been enticed into the army while under the influence of alcohol. To escape his enlistment he had to repay, within twenty-four hours of that attestation, his enlistment bounty (almost certainly already spent on drink), and to pay a further twenty shillings. The army was so unpopular with poor people of good character that families were often prepared to reduce themselves to beggary to find this smart money[13]. (It is interesting to reflect that despite all the changes over the century and a half since the time described, the army is still held in low regard in many working class circles, and the practice of buying-out is still current, though recruits now have a 'free' cooling-off period.)

It followed, inevitably, that in view of the type of person recruited, standards of physical fitness, intelligence and education were not, and could not be, high. There was not even a proper medical examination, and the recruit's declaration that he had no physical disability was accepted at face value. Checks were in fact so cursory that there are several well-documented instances of women enlisting by pretending to be male. Even the minimum age limit of sixteen was largely disregarded and boys of fourteen were often accepted.

Once enlisted, the recruit had to travel to the regiment's barracks or, if it was serving abroad, to the regimental depot. If a recruiting party had travelled far from their base this might be a considerable distance. Originally the recruit would have marched there, but in the mid-nineteenth century, with the coming of the

---

[13]*Ibid*

railways, it became normal to travel by train. Barracks were still a relatively new arrangement. In the early days soldiers were billeted on civilians, which was extremely unpopular with the latter, but a large building programme at the end of the eighteenth and through the nineteenth centuries - especially after the Crimean War - had made this rare in peacetime. In war it remained the solution when the number of troops in Great Britain was larger than the barrack space available, and was common as recently as the beginning of the Second World War. Many of the old barracks, and in particular some of those built shortly after the Crimean War, were still in use until the 1960s.[14]

At his barracks the recruit was issued with his kit, and training began. This was largely left to the non-commissioned officers, and the officer's life was largely one of idleness. (See the following pages). The soldier's training was extremely boring and consisted of the repetition of drill exercises, at first without arms, and after several weeks of that, with the musket. Up to eight hours a day might be spent in this way. In 1846 a recruit rose at five o'clock and 'made up' his bed (a term still in use over a century later: it means that the bed and bedding were prepared for inspection, with blankets folded precisely). This occupied a quarter of an hour. His toilet followed and at six he paraded for drill until a quarter to eight when he breakfasted. From ten till twelve there was drill again before dinner at one: meat (usually of the most wretched quality) and potatoes. At two there was more drill, until four o'clock. Unless he was on piquet the soldier was now free and could stroll in the vicinity of the barracks (he was not supposed to go more than one mile from them). Reading was popular

---

[14]The writer recalls being shown by his father, in 1955, the cavalry barracks at Aldershot in which the father had trained during the First World War. The barracks had been old then!

17

with those who could but most simply adjourned to the 'beer-shop' and drunkenness was inevitably common.[15] The cavalry also, of course, had to be trained to look after their horses and to ride. They first learnt how to march and to drill on foot. Then they learnt to use comb, sponge and brush, how to feed and water a horse, how to clean out the stables, saddling, unsaddling, and finally how to ride.

The barracks were not very comfortable. They were formed of long, narrow rooms in which beds were packed down the two long sides. In the centre was a coke burning stove. Windows were kept firmly shut at night, and if the stove did not burn properly, death from carbon monoxide poisoning was not unknown. At night soldiers relieved themselves in a large steel 'bucket' also in the centre of the room. The first bath in an English barracks was not installed until 1855, according to Neuberg.[16]

Most married soldiers also lived in barracks. Since 1817 regulations had permitted the accommodation in barracks of four married women per company of sixty men. A few regiments arranged this by providing a barrack room for several families to share, but more used the so-called 'corner system'. This involved the curtaining off of a corner of the ordinary barrack room, behind which the married couples and their children had little dignity or privacy. No furniture was provided until 1838 when beds and bedding were issued for the families. Nevertheless these women in barracks were fortunate compared with other soldiers' wives above the numerical limit who had to live in miserable lodgings in a nearby town, alone and away

---

[15]As described by (later) Staff Sergeant MacMullen and quoted in *Gone for a Soldier,* by Victor Neuberg, pub London 1989, an excellent study of life in the ranks from 1642 to recent times. p 27.
[16]See Neuberg, *op cit.*

from their husbands who were obliged to remain in barracks. No financial provision was made for these 'off-camp' families until 1848 when six married men per company were paid 1d (a fraction of a new penny) per day to live out of barracks. The position in Aldershot was even worse, for there families had originally to live in tents[17].

If a regiment was ordered overseas on operations, known as 'active service', most of the wives and families were left in an even worse position for then the number of 'official' wives permitted to travel with their husbands to the war was only a small proportion of the total. No provision at all was made for the rest. They were expected to return, destitute, to their original parishes for Poor Relief - almost impossible if, for example, that was in Ireland and the regiment was departing from the south of England. A good husband would try and save from his meagre pay and send the money home to wife and children, but this was not easy and for some unaccountable reason there was an Army Regulation which forbad this until three months after embarkation, enforcing a considerable delay before money could be sent even if it had been saved[18]. When the Crimean

---

[17]The reader is referred to Myra Trustram's scholarly study of the army wife in *Women of the Regiment, Marriage and the Victorian Army,* pub Cambridge, 1984.

[18]The writer cannot forbear to point out that in 1961 he was adjutant of 29th Field Regiment Royal Artillery which was ordered at very short notice to proceed urgently to Kuwait, then threatened by Iraq. In the event the threat was deterred by the speed and force of the British deployment and Iraq did not cross the international border. In barracks at the Royal Citadel, Plymouth, each married man had received his pay each week in cash at a pay parade, and paid over what was necessary to his wife for food and other family expenses. But there was no system for paying money to the wives of the soldiers

War started, this became a huge problem, and a Patriotic Fund was established to try and ease the hardships suffered by the families. Some of the letters published by the Fund as it tried to raise contributions from the public are heart-rending and how soldiers at the front maintained morale while their families starved at home is difficult to understand. The Secretary for War, Sidney Herbert, took a cold view of the problem, considering it better if the number of women allowed to go with their husbands was reduced from six per hundred men, to four, with the other two allowed half rations. He thought that 'this may seem very hard, but the more encouragement you give the soldier to marry the more you increase the evil which was now complained of'[19].

Improvements to the soldier's life came slowly, after determined efforts by a few far-sighted individuals, among whom one writer has suggested that 'the summit is held unassailably by the

---

who had been moved in emergency out of the UK, and it was weeks before any wife left behind even knew where her husband was, let alone received any money from him, far away in the Middle East. Our families were 'bailed out' by the wife of the commanding officer who drew on her own private funds and lent them to the 'abandoned' and financially-embarrassed soldiers' wives. As a result of that experience, new procedures were introduced, but that was over a hundred years after the outrageous treatment of wives now recorded.

[19]Quoted by Noel St John Williams in his comprehensive study of the army wife *Judy O'Grady and the Colonel's Lady* from *The Times* for 25 Feb 1854. Note how early the problem was presenting, for the first troops left England for the East only that same month.

abrasive and petulant 3rd Earl Grey'.[20] As Secretary at War from 1835-9 he pressed for good conduct awards, improved diets, better barracks, the rotation of battalions on tropical service, the building of barrack libraries and fives courts and the use of more locally recruited regiments in the colonies. Army schools for soldiers' children had been established in 1812, but in 1849 the education offered by army schoolmasters was extended to adult soldiers as well when a General Order required that all recruits must attend school for two hours a day. Other soldiers were allowed to attend if they wished. Except for a few enlightened regiments which by their own initiative introduced various measures including proper living accommodation for families, libraries and dry canteens for the men, such improvements were still far in the future. Meanwhile sutlers had been allowed to open canteens in barracks, paying the government a rent which they quickly recovered from the prices charged to the soldier. Regimental savings banks had been introduced in 1844 as an alternative to the canteens as a home for pay, but many soldiers had not the will power to resist the alcohol so freely and conveniently available. Nevertheless, in many regiments there was a paternal interest in the men and the efficiency of the unit. This was the driving force for officers and this lasted at least until the writer's own service and no doubt does still.

The need to police the Empire meant that the army, which had by 1850 reached some 110,000, (of which about 12,000 were cavalry, 90,000 infantry, 7,000 artillery and 1,200 engineers), was very thinly spread and nearly two-thirds was stationed abroad in India, the Mediterranean and the Colonies. About 20,000 were in Ireland and, at

---

[20]Hew Strachan in 'The early Victorian army and the nineteenth-century revolution in government', *The English Historical Review,* Vol 95 (1980).

home the garrison towns were occupied and the coast was defended. There were about one hundred regiments and these were quite individual and separate. There was no general staff and no divisional or brigade formations. Nominally the Crown was supreme, but in practice Parliament ruled, through the 'Secretary of State for War and the Colonies' [21]. Responsible to the latter, were the Commander-in-Chief (C-in-C), for Cavalry and Infantry; and the Master General of the Ordnance (MGO), for the two 'technical, or ordnance, corps', the Royal Artillery, and the Royal Engineers.[22] In fact the MGO, responsible for the provision of armaments and explosives as well as the two corps mentioned, prepared his own estimates and was responsible for these direct to Parliament, which provided a source of friction with the Secretary of State, as did his responsibility for the ordnance corps with the Commander- in-Chief.

Both C-in-C and MGO each had crucial control over officer appointments and promotions in their respective spheres. In 'the ordnance corps' officers were appointed only after passing the entrance examination for the Royal Military Academy, Woolwich (nicknamed 'the Shop'), satisfactorily completing the course there, and passing the final examinations. Between 1825 and 1849 a quarter of those admitted failed to gain commissions, most of them for academic, not disciplinary reasons[23]. Thereafter, in those corps promotion was by seniority. There was no purchase of first

---

[21]For a full discussion of the constitutional position, see JSAHR, vol 52, p221 et seq, for the excellent article by the late Lieutenant Colonel H. Moyse-Bartlett on that aspect and on the army of 1850 generally.
[22]At that time the Royal Engineers were an officer-only corps, and the men were all in the Royal Sappers and Miners. The latter were incorporated in the former in 1856.
[23]Recorded in Moyse-Bartlett's article mentioned at note 2 above.

commissions, nor of subsequent 'steps'. This unfortunately substituted another drawback in place of the one avoided: if indeed the purchase system was a drawback - see below. In the ordnance corps promotion depended on 'dead men's shoes', and so inordinate lengths of time were spent in the junior ranks. In the Crimea it is recorded that Lord Raglan, commanding the Army of the East, recognised Dacres, a gunner officer, then a colonel, whom he had known as a junior officer when Raglan had been MGO. 'How are you getting on, Dacres?' his lordship is said to have enquired. Dacres replied 'My lord, when a man has been twenty years a subaltern, he can never be said to be getting on...' Dacres had been commissioned from Woolwich in December 1817 and was promoted Second Captain in December 1837.

In the cavalry and infantry, including the Guards, the purchase system applied. First commissions required the approval of the C-in-C, but only from 1849 had a simple examination to be passed. This was largely due to Lord Grey, the reformer, who had returned as Secretary for War and the Colonies in 1846 with more ideas, including such an examination: not to show a professional qualification for entry, but simply to confirm that the applicant had the education of a gentleman, to ensure a minimum level of competence in the army. This involved writing fluently and well, arithmetic, geometry and trigonometry, history, geography, Latin, French or German, and the principles of the British Constitution. But it was considered far more important by Wellington and his peers that the young man should be a good shot and a fearless cross-country rider. Grey also introduced promotion examinations for officers. In these ideas he was joined by Sir Charles Trevelyan, the energetic and influential assistant secretary at the Treasury. Both ideas were initially opposed by Wellington, but all were implemented before the great man's death. (In passing one may note that other policies pursued by

Trevelyan were much less helpful and it was he who had obstructed the revival of the commissariat when in 1850 Lord Somerset, later Lord Raglan, the military secretary, and the Adjutant General, Sir George Brown, had pointed out that there was not one ready for the field. Trevelyan was sure that should a British army take the field a body of well-trained commissariat officers would be ready to perform the necessary services, and - an ominous codicil in view of later events - 'to keep in check the lavish expenditure which has generally been incurred at the commencement of a campaign.')[24] Only one technical subject - fortification - was included in the qualifying examination and there was no need to attend the Royal Military College at Sandhurst to acquire the rudimentary knowledge required to pass and only a few did attend there or a 'private' military college, of which there were several. Thereafter, when an officer wished to sell out, the promotion or 'step' could be purchased by the most senior officer in the next rank below. If he could not, or would not, pay then the officer next below him in seniority could buy the promotion, and so on. Thus no one could be promoted over the head of a senior except by purchase, and not then if the senior was himself prepared to pay. First commissions were not necessarily by purchase: those passing out top from Sandhurst paid no price; and vacancies sometimes arose due to expansion of the establishment, or the death of a serving officer. A deserving man could then be appointed, without purchase, to the vacancy by the C-in-C's patronage. Death, and expansion of the establishment, applied to vacancies in higher ranks as well. The most senior officer was then promoted, and in this way, in time, the more able officers slowly reached the senior ranks - a good example being Sir Colin Campbell, later Lord Clyde, of Crimean and Indian Mutiny fame. The impecunious officer longed for war to carry off some of his seniors, and this rather callous approach,

---

[24]See Hew Strachan's essay referred to at footnote 18.

epitomized in the traditional young officers' toast of 'A bloody war or a sickly season!'[25], is also seen in several officers' letters and journals as the Crimean War began a few years later. (So, one must note, is the rudimentary level of education - if one can judge by punctuation - shown by most officers, young and more senior.)

The purchase system meant, of course, that the vast majority of officers in the Guards, cavalry and infantry, were drawn from a particular social class. (Although the so-called 'ordnance corps', the Royal Artillery and Royal Engineers, had no purchase system the social class from which their officers were drawn was not very different, although the need to pass an examination to get in, and more examinations to pass out successfully, did deter some upper class candidates.) The British fear of military despotism, seen during the Protectorate of Cromwell, and something very similar under Charles I and James II, meant that the composition of the army officer corps, unlike that of the navy, was of great political significance. The Royal Navy could promote men from the lower deck, commission foreigners, and act much as they chose - for they posed no threat to the state. On the contrary, Parliament was traditionally committed to army officers being of 'high social position, holding large possessions and attached to the Protestant succession'.[26] It was thought that such officers would pose little threat to the political status quo for they had more to lose from revolution. Wellington was in no doubt. The officer, in his opinion, 'should be a gentleman, a man of "education", manners, honour, and other qualities acquired by the education which English gentlemen receive... This is the man to whom all look in

---

[25]Moyse Bartlett, *op cit*, p231.
[26]Quoted by CB Otley in his article, 'The Social Origins of British Army Officers', in *The Sociological Review,* Vol 18, no 2 (1970).

moments of difficulty and danger.'[27] The danger of men entering for economic reasons, 'military adventurers', was guarded against by the derisory pay which officers received. Even as late as 1869 it was still what it had been in the reign of William III (1689)! It was impossible for an officer to live on it. Typically about half of his pay would be due to the mess for dinners alone. Private means were an absolute necessity.[28] However as the nineteenth century went forward the proportion of nobility and landed gentry in the officer corps fell slowly but steadily and a new 'middle' class, still wealthy, sons of the professions - clergymen, lawyers, doctors and army officers - came to provide the majority. The author of an article containing a detailed study of fathers of new entrants to the Royal Military College at Sandhurst has pointed out that until 1871 attendance there was not compulsory, and he estimates that in peace-time three quarters of new commissions went by purchase to young men who had not bothered to attend the college.[29] It seems reasonable to assume that this group would be less inclined to study their profession, and might be more inclined to leave boring matters such as daily drill to others.... A new group also came to provide candidates for commissions: the successful businessman of the Industrial Revolution, seeking the instant increase in social status brought by having a son in the army - especially in a fashionable, and therefore expensive, regiment. This did produce some tension between the old and the new, but this was not based on class distinction so much as resentment by some of the sons of clergymen, lawyers and army officers (many of whom had traditionally sent their sons to be officers) because increasingly such fathers could not afford the cost of commissions and uniforms for

---

[27]Strachan, *op cit.*
[28]Otley, *op cit.* He quotes WilliamII, surely a typographical error for William III.
[29]Otley, *op cit.*

their offspring as could the nouveau riche businessman. Underlying this resentment there was also a widespread feeling that such new officers did not understand the finer points of the community in a landed society. William Napier, brother of Sir Charles, wrote: 'a man of high breeding is hand in glove with his men, while the son of a millionaire hardly speaks to a soldier.'[30] A modern author has pointed out that just as the private soldier, recruited from the very poorest and most ignorant, was not typical of his civilian brothers, nor did the officer corps[31] reflect the great changes which had taken place in British society, and as both officers and men were recruited from unrepresentative social groups, the nation as a whole had little directly to do with the army[32]. Perhaps one may add: in peacetime, as little as possible. Finally, this shift in officer recruiting led to an emphasis on snobbery and elitism based on wealth and ostentation rather than military merit and encapsulated in the so-called 'crack cavalry regiment' to which the very rich migrated.[33] Some were aristocrats with new found wealth due to coal or somesuch being discovered and developed on their land: others were sons of businessmen who had become landowners with country estates. Inevitably less wealthy officers, in less fashionable regiments, aped their smart counterparts as far as their means, or the credit they could obtain from tradesmen, allowed. Army officers generally became ever more stiff-necked and

---

[30]Quoted by Strachan, *op cit.*

[31]Correlli Barnett in his *Britain and her Army* correctly points out that this is a misnomer for there was no such 'corps', but instead many different, tight and exclusive little circles of separate regimental messes.

[32]Correlli Barnett, *Britain and her Army,* pub 1970.

[33]Alan J Guy, *Oeconomy and Discipline,* pub 1985.

haughty, rigid in social etiquette and distinctions, dominated by a hierarchy of birth, wealth, kinship, connections and fashion[34].

It will be little surprise therefore that there was no reversal in the decline in many regiments, seen as early as the 1780s, to the attention given to the drudgery attendant on daily command. A whole range of duties which in European armies were the province of subalterns, including the task of maintaining regimental accounts, was delegated to non-commissioned officers while the young gentlemen searched for diversion elsewhere.[35] Even the appointment of adjutant, which needed a thorough knowledge of drill and the field exercises, (based on *Field Exercises and Evolutions of the Army* originally drafted by Dundas but modified somewhat from experience in the Peninsular War), was in many regiments passed to a 'commissioned ranker'. The adjutant's principal duty was to act as assistant to the major, superintending the drilling of recruits, issuing orders to the sergeants, supervising punishments imposed by regimental courts-martial, compiling monthly returns and having custody of the regiment's books. It can be seen that it would have little appeal to an indigent subaltern.

Of course, every regiment was inspected annually by a general officer[36]. This had been instituted in 1716 as a direct extension of the royal commitment to personal inspections which had been carried out enthusiastically by George I, his son, and the Duke of Cumberland. The last had been particularly strict and his inspections were an unnerving prospect for a commanding officer who had any doubts about the fitness of his unit. Annual circuits had been instituted in

---

[34]Barnett, p282.
[35]Guy, *op cit.*
[36]*Ibid,* p32.

about 1720 and procedures were intensified and extended in scope after 1748. The first question was a regiment's preparedness. The general would require units to pass in review order before them, noting how well drilled the soldiers and horses were, and the condition of their clothing, weapons and equipment. They would be put through the manual exercise of arms and parade evolutions, with any mistakes or shortcomings being noted, and the general would exhort the officers to perfect their knowledge and that of their men and to improve discipline of both. The unit administration was then checked in great detail. Had the soldiers been punctually and properly paid, without any uncalled-for 'stoppages' (deductions from pay - a term still used)? Were their clothing, arms and equipment in good order? Finally a detailed report was made, originally to the king himself. Gradually additional financial responsibilities were added, in the first place to ensure that the number of men corresponded with the paymaster's books, and as years passed the financial aspects became more and more important and the inspecting general became far more concerned with the state of accounts, arms and uniforms, than the military preparedness which had been the original reason for the inspection. (Readers who have served since the Second World War will recognise the 'Annual Administrative Inspection', with its shortcomings, and its opportunities, nay challenges, to conceal minor blemishes from the inspecting general and his team...)

Then in 1853 for perhaps the first time ever in peace, it was planned to exercise the individual regiments with others in brigade and division formation, and with other arms. This was largely to be a show of strength against the French for great alarm had been caused when Louis Napoleon had proclaimed himself Napoleon III, Emperor of France. A special camp of instruction was duly set up at Chobham in Surrey and command was given to General Lord Seaton, formerly John Colborn, who had fought at Maida, in the Peninsula and at

Waterloo. He had earlier commanded the 52nd Foot, where he had insisted on all his officers knowing the field exercises thoroughly, practising them in turn with the whole battalion[37]. This was not the normal practice with other regiments.

Daily life for officers serving at home - other than the adjutant and regimental staff - involved occasional demands for their service at some review or manoeuvre, but for the most part was spent on field sports, looking after their horses and shooting, and the social whirl in town. Of course this life of racing, polo, hunting, balls and parties required an income much greater than an officer's pay, but it was all very agreeable and undemanding[38]. It was centred around the Officers' Mess. After the foundation of the first such for the Royal Artillery at Woolwich[39], several regiments formed them in the second half of the eighteenth century though it took some fifty years for them to become compulsory. Bennett Cuthbertson who produced in 1776 a treatise on 'the complete interior management and economy of a battalion of infantry' wrote that it was 'incumbent on the colonel to contrive every method in his power for the establishment of a mess, at which all the Officers, without distinction of Rank (for these should never subsist between Gentlemen, except on Duty), can be properly and genteelly accommodated, ... within an Ensign's pay..., living always together as one family, (which) must surely strengthen the bands of friendship between individuals, and unite the whole in that sort of harmony and affection, which in a well regulated Corps ought

---

[37]See Frederick Myatt, *The British Infantry 1660-1945,* p112.
[38]*Beggars in Red,* John Strawson, p 136.
[39]Sadly now vacated by the Royal Regiment after over 200 years' continuous occupation.

ever to subsist, and without which every thing goes wrong.'[40] By the middle of the nineteenth century the reality was somewhat different. An officer in a Scottish regiment wrote in 1857 that 'the officers of the British army are nearly all gentlemen, and many of them are highly accomplished; some few, however, have their faults'. He went on to allege that in most regiments the junior officers regularly brought prostitutes into barracks, openly and in full view of the sentries who themselves could be severely punished for even speaking to a whore in the streets. Senior officers were aware of this but did nothing. Although the writer thought the subalterns, for the most part, a fine spirited set of young men, they attended little to the study of their profession, learnt expensive habits and vicious pursuits, ran up bills they couldn't pay and devoted a great deal of their time to the seduction of innocent and uneducated girls.[41] This was a picture of the army which would not have been believed by the general public if they had learnt of it even a few years earlier.

Such was the British army in 1854 as we take up the story in Windsor...

---

[40]Quoted in FstC Vivian's article 'John André as a Young Officer', *JSAHR,* Vol 40, (1962)
[41]Quoted by Lt Col H Moyse-Bartlett in 'The British army in 1850', *JSAHR,* Vol 52, (1954)

THE WINDSOR COURTS-MARTIAL

Chapter 2 - Conduct Unbecoming an Officer and a Gentleman

Robert Garrett, the commanding officer of the 46th Foot, a typical English line regiment, not particularly fashionable, was far from pleased when he was told by his adjutant early on the morning of 29th June, 1854, that an unpleasant incident between two of his young officers had taken place in the Officers' Mess during the previous night and that it had resulted in one of the officers receiving serious head injuries, needing the attention of the regimental Assistant Surgeon. Already warned for the Army of the East, and hoping that at last his service might be marked by recognition and advancement, Garrett was irritable at any distraction. Further, the army's Adjutant General had but recently sent round to all commanding officers a strong note about the behaviour of officers. Any incident in his battalion was bound to reflect on Garrett and might well prejudice his progress: a bitter blow after all the patience he had shown since he had served in Wellington's army in the Peninsular War. For Garrett was indeed a Peninsular veteran in the army of 1854, and while there were several of these in the higher ranks - Raglan, the Commander-in-Chief himself, for example - few were still serving, as he was, in the relatively low rank for his age of Lieutenant Colonel. Surely he would soon attract the attention of his superiors and receive the promotion he felt he deserved? But not if he was noticed because his regiment had disgraced itself because its officers did not know how to behave.

He sighed when he heard that Perry was the culprit. This young man was not from the same social class as his brother officers and this had already caused problems. Perry was the son of a Paymaster, now serving in India, and had obtained his commission as an ensign without purchase when the establishment had been increased: an unknown senior officer's patronage had obtained the vacancy for Perry, as a gesture of appreciation to his father, who had probably been a good NCO known to the senior officer before being commissioned as Paymaster. This last was not a highly regarded position in any regiment and was thought but slightly above the soldiers as regards social class. It was bad enough for the 46th to have this fellow, with his very different background and lack of means, without him behaving in a disgraceful manner and, apparently, attacking another officer. Greer, who had been attacked was of parentage and upbringing above reproach. Perry had been confined by the adjutant in close arrest the night before - in effect that meant another officer had sat with him in his room all night, and was with him now. His meal had been served to him on a tray in his room, and the escort had also eaten there. The regiment's ensigns had been placed on a roster to act as escort, a task none cared for, as Perry had no close friends in the regiment and few had found his company agreeable. Apart from his rather serious and pious character he lacked the means to join in those activities which involved spending money, and what amusing activity did not? However Garrett looked on the bright side. Surely this was a way to get rid of Perry, who clearly did not fit in the 46th, which though perhaps not the smartest of line infantry regiments still had its standards. Garrett wrote immediately to the Major General commanding the district recommending that Perry be courtmartialled for the dastardly assault.

Courts-martial in the 1850s

In 1854 the annual Army Act which until 1976 governed army discipline, and which needed to be passed by Parliament each year (a relic of the days when Parliament did not trust the army, and felt more secure if they were able to consider its legislative standing and authority each year) had not been introduced and the governing legislation was the Mutiny Act, introduced in 1689 and renewed annually, and the Articles of War, which governed discipline in detail. The Mutiny Act had changed little since the days of Marlborough and private soldiers were sometimes still flogged for misdemeanours which would strike most modern readers as trivial. Not long before, in 1846, there had been a national outcry when Private White of the 7th Queen's Own Hussars had died shortly after receiving 150 lashes for the offence of 'insubordination'. Although a regimental autopsy reported that death was due to a defect of the heart and was 'in no way connected with the corporal punishment' this was not accepted by the general public and there were outcries in the radical press. Thus, led by the newspapers then read only by the influential elite, the House of Commons again considered abolition of the practice, but the house contained too many ex-officers who considered corporal punishment the only way to maintain discipline in an army composed of the refuse of human society. The maximum punishment was however reduced to fifty lashes. It was another thirty-five years before flogging was abolished in the army.

Officers were not, of course, subject to such corporal punishment, and Commanding Officers were not themselves able to deal with any serious offence they committed. Minor indiscretions were usually the subject of extra duty, but a real offence would require a report to the general commanding the district concerned and he would in his turn report to the

Commander- in-Chief who could then order a general court-martial. This would be under the Presidency of a senior officer with twelve other officers of varying rank down to that of the accused to assist him. An experienced - but not normally legally qualified - Judge Advocate, or Deputy Judge Advocate, would normally be attached to the court to ensure that everything done was in accordance with the law and with army instructions. President, Judge Advocate and members of the court were all appointed by the C-in-C who was known as the convening officer. The regiment of the accused would supply the prosecutor, and the accused, already described emotively as the 'prisoner' and symbolically deprived of his sword, could have a brother officer to help him defend himself. The procedure was very broadly similar to that in a civil court, with the very important differences that no lawyer might speak for the accused, and the defence were not even allowed directly to cross-examine the witnesses called by the prosecution. Proposed questions had to be put to the court in writing. If they approved of them, and they might well not, the President would put them to the witnesses. If the court did not approve of the proposed question, then it could not, and would not, be put. The army thought that the proceedings were private, and though the public were admitted to the courts it was thought that there could be no newspaper reports of what transpired. This was to be the first shock to the establishment...

Chapter 3 - Proceedings begin

And so, on Wednesday 13th July 1854, the General Court Martial assembled in the Mess Room at the Infantry Barracks, Windsor.

The district Major General had earlier forwarded Colonel Garrett's recommendation to the Horse Guards where the Adjutant General had consulted the Judge Advocate General for advice on the charges to be preferred. In replying[42], S.C. Denison, the Deputy Judge Advocate General, suggested that it might be advisable, before putting Perry on trial, to ascertain that Greer was out of danger as the evidence submitted showed that the case might 'be one in which it would be proper to send the prisoner for trial before a court of ordinary jurisdiction' - presumably foreseeing a charge of manslaughter, or murder to be tried in a civil court. In the event, Greer was not nearly so badly injured as Garrett had made out, and the court sat as planned.

The President was Colonel the Hon James Lindsay MP of the Grenadier Guards and the twelve other members were drawn from several regiments stationed nearby, but not of course the 46th. Brevet Colonel William Slater was from the Depot at Windsor, Lieutenant Colonel George Grey Rous from the Grenadier Guards, and Lieutenant Colonel W. Mark Wood from the Coldstream Guards. There was one major, William Custance

---

[42] WO93/13 Judge Advocate General's: Ordinary Letter Book 1850-56

from the 6th Dragoon Guards, and two Brevet Majors: the Hon Fenton J. Freke of the 2nd Life Guards and Thomas Bridge of the 84th. Six captains came from six different regiments. Senior was H.E.Montresor of the Grenadiers, next F.Synge of the 43rd Foot and the Hon D.C.Fitzgerald de Ros of the 1st Life Guards, then J.H.L.Contour of the Coldstream, R.J.Raynes of the 28th and last WilliamRickman of the 77th. Two lieutenants, Perry's own rank, made up the final two places: Henry William Dennie of the 28th and William Henry Mansfield of the 44th.

Major Arthur John Pack, 7th Fusiliers, Assistant Adjutant General, acted as Deputy Judge Advocate, and Mr Darvill, a solicitor and Town Clerk of Windsor, was present as the accused's professional adviser but was unable to speak.

Some time later, when the public interest in the proceedings was at fever-pitch, *The Times* described the scene as follows. At one end of the Infantry Barracks at Windsor, where the 46th Regiment was quartered, beside and looking into the barrack-yard there was a ground floor room, somewhat long, and papered with green striped paper. It was the mess room of the barracks. It contained a dining table large enough for sixteen to dine and at one end sat the President with seven members of the Court down each side. All were in full uniform. To the President's right were three bay windows and in one bay sat the Deputy Judge Advocate. Before him there was a small table with writing materials and a red book - presumably some work on Court-martial law. Opposite him, in a dark corner close to the President's left hand sat the Prosecutor at a small round table. At the end of the table opposite to the President there was another small table and there sat young Perry, in uniform, and his legal adviser, Mr Darvill. At the furthest window from the Deputy Judge Advocate there was another table for one or two reporters taking notes. There were two orderly sergeants with their caps on, constantly employed in carrying bits of paper about the court. There were two doors, one at each end, and in the barrack yard outside stood those waiting to be called as witnesses.

Pack read the order assembling the court and the warrants appointing the President and himself as Deputy Judge Advocate, and the accused - referred to throughout as the prisoner - confirmed that he had no objection to the President or any of the members who were then sworn in.

Pack then read the charge which alleged that Perry had been guilty of conduct unbecoming an officer and gentleman, and to the prejudice of good order and military discipline, in having at Windsor, on or about the night of the 28th June, or morning of the 29th, committed an outrageous assault on Lieutenant Thomas Fergus Greer, of the 46th Regiment, and grievously wounded him, by beating him on the head and face with a pair of candlesticks. Perry, asked to plead, answered quietly but firmly 'Not Guilty' and the prosecution case began.

Most modern readers will react with some surprise to the identity of the prosecuting officer - none other than Perry's commanding officer himself, Lieutenant Colonel Robert Garrett.

The first witness was Greer, the subject of the attack, and he was examined by the Deputy Judge Advocate. He told the court: 'I was in Lieutenant Perry's room on the morning of the 29th of June and had an altercation with him. I was rather excited. I pulled him about, when he, without giving me any warning, seized a candlestick from the table and struck me a violent blow on the head, which rendered me insensible. When I was sufficiently recovered I went towards him, and he again struck me on the head. I remember nothing more, until having recovered, for the second time, I told him to send for the doctor, which he did. This took place in the barracks at Windsor.'

Pack then announced that throughout the trial, if either prosecuting officer, or prisoner, wished to put a question to any witness they must put it in writing and hand it to the President for the court to decide if it might be put, and for the President to ask the question himself, if his colleagues approved it.

In this way Colonel Garrett asked Greer if he had been seriously wounded by the blows he had received and where on his person they had been inflicted. Greer said on the left side of his head, and yes, he had been seriously wounded.

Perry then asked, in the same tortuous way, if he Greer had been in the billiard room on the night of the 28th when Perry had been playing with Ensigns Hutton and Helyer, and if Greer had asked them to finish quickly so that Greer could play. Greer agreed.

Perry's next written question was however to cause the President to ask him what was the drift of his questions as the court could not consider any previous altercation, and the President thought that the court would consider it, but would probably not allow it. Perry explained that it was necessary to his defence to elicit every circumstance of the quarrel and to show that, by word and manner, Greer had threatened to assault him, justifying the violence afterwards used by Perry. The court was cleared and the members discussed, and then allowed, the question. Had Greer asked Ensign Hutton to play, and had Hutton refused? Greer could not recollect. He did agree that Perry had volunteered to play with him, had won the game, and then at Greer's solicitation had tossed a coin for 'double or quits' which

Perry had also won, so that Greer owed him five shillings altogether.

Perry then sought to ask if Greer had come into the anteroom between 1 and 2 o'clock with a woman, had tossed Perry for a bottle of wine and won, and had then asked Perry and Captain O'Toole to come to his room to drink the wine, and see his woman. The court was again cleared and on re-assembly the President said that the question should not be answered. The prisoner must confine himself to shaking the evidence of the witness and he would have the opportunity to bring other things forward when he presented his defence.

Perry said that he had but one combined case and the questions were put to shake the evidence of the witness. With respect he thought he was entitled, according to the law of England, to ask any questions in cross examination. He referred the court to *Simmons on Court-Martials*[43]

The President said that the only authority recognised by the court was the Mutiny Act. While they wished to give the prisoner every indulgence, they felt bound to confine themselves to the point at issue. Perry substituted other questions and Greer

---

[43] This book was a forerunner of the modern *Manual of Military Law* familiar to those who have served in recent times. It was not, however, an official publication but had been written originally in 1830 by Thomas Frederick Simmons, a half pay Royal Artillery captain and was revised from time to time when there were significant amendments to the Mutiny Act. Thus a second edition was published in 1835 and after Simmons' death, his son Frederick, also Captain, revised it for a third edition in 1843 and again for a fourth published in 1852. It was this 1852 edition which was current at the time of Perry's trial.

agreed that when Perry was in Greer's room Perry had reluctantly agreed to give Greer the chance to recover his losses by playing cards. When cards could not be found, a roulette box had been produced, but Perry had said that he did not understand the game. Greer had insisted that he play, and Perry had won again and again until Greer owed him one hundred shillings. When Perry had left and gone to his own room, Greer had followed him and dragged him back by the collar. They played again, and again Perry won. Greer had then followed Perry to his room and called him a 'son of a ----' and 'a swindler'. This last question Greer refused to answer and the President intervened to ask if it was necessary to persist in such questions which were all of the same character. Perry said that he was attempting to show the provocation he had suffered. He had been most forebearing and had at last struck in self defence. He hoped that he would be able to give evidence himself on oath but the President said that he could not as no power to do so was given by the Mutiny Act.

More questions from Perry to Greer followed and Perry put to Greer that the latter was the stronger man and that he had only struck, while within Greer's grasp, in self defence. Greer denied this and that Perry had been within his grasp when he had struck.

The court established from Greer that the incident had taken place between 2 and 3 o'clock in the morning, and the next witness, Assistant Surgeon Charles Carroll Dempster then explained how at about half past 4 o'clock in the morning he was awakened by Perry who asked him to go at once to his room where he found Greer leaning forward against the table, his face and a great portion of his head covered with blood which was flowing freely from several wounds. Perry told Dempster that he had done it when Greer had entered his room and insulted him. Perry had ordered Greer into arrest, but Greer refused and insulted him again. Perry had then struck him. Dempster had taken Greer to his own room, dressed his wounds and put him to bed. There had been nine wounds, all on the scalp and all contused and lacerated as if from a blunt instrument. Two were dangerous, and the others comparatively slight.

The adjutant, Lieutenant Charles Somerville M'Alester, produced the regimental register and formally proved that Perry was 21 years and 11 months old, and had served one year and five months in the regiment. He then told the court that he had been asked by Colonel Garrett to inquire into the incident on the morning after it had taken place. He had placed both officers under arrest. Accompanied by the sergeant major, he had found and taken possession of one candlestick in Perry's room - broken and bloodstained, and Perry had produced the other, also broken and marked with blood, when asked for it. They were silver plated and very heavy. Greer had a very swollen head when arrested, with one of his eyes nearly closed up but Perry bore no marks that M'Alester could see. Perry put to him that he had shown him the bruise on his chest the next day, but M'Alester remembered him opening his shirt, but could not remember what any marks were like.

The court adjourned for the day, reassembling at 11 o'clock the next day. Now another Windsor solicitor, Mr G.H.Long, was present to watch on behalf of Greer.

The second day - Greer's 'woman' appears

As soon as the court assembled, the Deputy Judge Advocate said that he had received a letter from Perry, arguing that under the statutes 6th and 7th William IV he was entitled to be represented by counsel or attorney. The application was recorded, and denied. A court martial did not allow the accused to have a legal adviser. A military or personal friend might assist them but it was not the custom of war, nor according to the practice of courts martial, to allow a prisoner to appear by counsel.

A Miss Esther Major was then called and sworn. She told the court that she was a dressmaker by trade but was in Greer's room in the barracks between 1 and 2 o'clock on the night concerned. She had seen Greer and Perry play at *rouge et noir* and Perry win, though she thought that after early wins Greer had recovered all his losses but five shillings. She confirmed that Perry had repeatedly wished to stop, but Greer had insisted that he continue, repeatedly breaking his promise that they play a certain number of times and Perry then be allowed to go. She had heard Greer use very offensive terms to Perry but then both had gone on talking and laughing. When Perry had returned to his room she had heard him say 'Leave go of me, and leave my room.' She had also heard Greer call Perry 'a son of a ----', and other offensive terms while playing in Greer's room. Before this last evidence of Greer's conduct, the Judge Advocate General had expressed the doubt that any amount of provocation would justify the assault which had taken place.

Perry now called two witnesses, first M'Alester the adjutant, who confirmed that he had never personally had reason to complain of Perry's conduct and that he had always conducted himself as a gentleman but, he added that he had lately been censured by the commanding officer. Captain and Paymaster Corcoran also testified that Perry had always conducted himself properly and had often shown great control of temper and good feeling. So the second day ended.

The third day - contempt of court?

The third day began with a solemn announcement by the President. He had seen in several of the London papers that morning the publication of the proceedings of the previous two days. At the very start of proceedings he had expressly forbidden any publication of the evidence until the case was closed. Without accusing anyone, he considered publication a contempt of the court and the Deputy Judge Advocate agreed saying that the offending parties were liable to proceedings under the Mutiny Act and Articles of War. Mr Darvill, Perry's adviser, and the editor of the local paper sprang to deny any part in the publication, but *The Times* in reporting the remarks of President and Deputy Judge Advocate commented as follows: 'The court is open. Not a tittle of evidence can be received within closed doors; and no reporter who knew his duty would consider himself bound by an order which the Court had no right to make, and no power to enforce.'

Nor had *The Times* finished there: there was a forceful leading article on the subject of the trial, but this was published, with the account of the third day, on the fourth day, after the hearings had been concluded. More of this anon, but for the moment, we return to the third day...

First the Deputy Judge Advocate addressed Perry. He told him that due to his youth and short experience of service that he was Perry's adviser as much as the court's. The court would have to consider if it would allow Perry to enter into matters calculated to criminate others, and totally irrelevant to the point at issue. He warned that he might have to interrupt such matters, but that this was not prejudice against Perry, but only a sense of duty.

Perry's Defence

Perry began to read his defence. He told how he had joined the regiment at the Linenhall Barracks, Dublin on 14th of April, 1853. Later the regiment had moved to the Royal Barracks, also in Dublin, and then to Cork and finally Windsor. Apart from a period on detachment in December 1853, and three weeks' leave in March 1854, Perry had been with the regiment throughout. He explained that he was the son of Paymaster C.J. Perry of the 87th Royal Irish Fusiliers, presently in India. His mother was dead and he had no close relative to whom he could turn: he was entirely dependent upon strangers for advice and kindly sympathy. At this point Perry became much affected. When he joined the regiment his means were limited and he was personally unwilling, and pecuniarly unable, to indulge in excesses. He was therefore what is called a 'quiet man' and the object of laughter and reproach among many in the regiment. But he thought it better to pay his way and live in good credit with peace of mind, than to ruin his prospects in life by heavy expenditure which his father's means would not justify. While in Dublin he had once been betrayed into an act of gambling and had lost fifty shillings. He had resolved never to gamble again and apart from whist or cribbage for a few points with a brother officer he had kept this resolution until the unhappy events described in the trial. Even then he stressed that he had not played with any hope of winning, but under duress to give Greer an opportunity of recovering his losses. Far from that result, however, Greer had lost again and again, and now owed Perry two hundred and sixty pounds. Perry had not received, and did not expect to receive, one farthing of that sum. He hoped that in view of his previous good conduct, and as he was not a habitual gambler, the court would not be prejudiced against him for the gambling which had taken place on the night concerned. He was not an ungenerous, ill-natured or quarrelsome man and had patiently borne many provocations. Time after time he had been

46

dragged from his bed at all hours of the night, and in a state of nudity had been compelled to go through the sword exercises before the officers of his own and other regiments. He had appealed to his superiors but had met with no redress, on the contrary, everything but what he had a right to expect. As a man he had felt degraded, as a gentleman dishonoured and as a subaltern friendless and alone. He had patiently and silently submitted. Despite the ignominies practised upon him he had not resented nor borne any ill-will against his fellow officers. He had accepted his destiny and had hoped that in time he might rise in his profession and maintain an honourable position in the service to which he had become attached.

He said that the true facts of the night 28/29 June were as follows. He was in the billiard room playing with Ensigns Hutton and Helyer when Greer arrived and asked them to finish quickly so that he could play. When they had finished Greer asked Hutton to play, but he would not and Perry volunteered, and they played for five shillings. Greer won. They played again, Greer betting Perry ten shillings to one shilling that he would win again, and he did. Perry owed him six shillings. They played a third time, now for one pound. Perry won. They went on playing and at the end Perry owed Greer six shillings. At Greer's suggestion they tossed for double or quits. After several tossings at Greer's insistence, Perry had won five pounds. Greer already owed five pounds from an earlier loan and now owed ten pounds. While they played Greer frequently cursed Perry's luck. Perry now refused to play further and went to the anteroom where other officers were sitting. Some time afterwards Greer came in with a woman, now known to be Esther Major. She went upstairs to Greer's room. Greer asked Perry to toss for a bottle of wine for his woman. Perry did, and lost. He ordered a bottle of sherry and Greer asked him and Captain O'Toole to join him and the woman to drink it.

47

They went upstairs, where Greer demanded revenge for the money he had lost and asked for playing cards. None could be found in the mess and Greer then produced a small box with a pea in it, called a roulette-box. Despite Perry's protestations that he did not know the game, 'black and red', Greer insisted that he play. Perry was reluctant as he remembered once in Dublin how Greer had kept him and others playing until six in the morning so that he could recover money he had at first lost. The whole management of the box was by Greer, but this time Perry won repeatedly, and the woman said Greer was unlucky. Greer cursed him and Perry objected to his language and said he would play no longer. Greer pushed him back in his chair, and they played on. Several times Greer promised that they would only play a few times more, each time declaring 'On my word as an officer and a gentleman, this shall be the last turn' but each time breaking this promise. When they were nearly equal, Greer said that Perry was the best fellow in the world, but the scales tipped again and soon Greer was very much down once more. His language became disgusting. Perry got up and went to his own room, but Greer followed him and pulled him by the coat out into the corridor, and Perry returned reluctantly to the game. He won again, until Greer owed one hundred and ten pounds - [then, of course, an enormous sum] - and became very agitated. He now used the offensive language reported to the court earlier. Perry left his room and as he did so, Greer followed and on the stairs caught hold of his coat. Perry continued to return to his own room, and there thinking to elude Greer's grasp, he slipped out of his coat. Greer seized him by the waistcoat and pummelled him. He then told him to go through the sword exercises, but changed his mind and said he would bet fifty pounds that Perry could not with a single sword stroke slice a candle in two. Perry protested at this, but finally agreed and was successful. Greer grew angrier. He now bet a hundred pounds that Perry could not slice a smaller candle on the table in two. Perry was again successful. Greer then attacked him ferociously, catching him by the waistcoat, placing both hands through the armholes and hurting Perry severely. He threw him several times upon his bed and against the wall, hurting his shoulders and head. He asked how much he owed. When Perry told him it was now two hundred and sixty pounds, Greer renewed his foul language, adding 'swindler' to his earlier insults. Perry had ordered him out of his room, when he refused to go had said he would report him to the commanding officer, and then told him he was under arrest. Greer said he would see Perry ---- first. He continued to thrust him back and forwards, and threatened to strike him in the face. Perry told him that to do so would cost him his commission. He then struck Perry several more blows on the chest and stomach and as he did so, Perry reached behind him and grasped the candlestick. He struck Greer one blow on the head, breaking the candlestick, but he could not get Greer off him and, realizing how much stronger Greer was than he, seized the other candlestick and hit him until he let go. Greer then told Perry to go for the doctor and he did so. Greer was taken to his own room.

Perry said he had offered to give evidence on oath but this had been refused by the court. Only Greer and Perry, and to a slight extent the woman Esther Major, could say what had happened. Greer had refused to answer the material questions, and Esther Major had heard only part of what had transpired. Greer had admitted the altercation, and that he had got excited, and pulled Perry about. He had said that Perry's blow had rendered him insensible, but also that he had told Perry to fetch the doctor. Both the doctor and Esther Major had confirmed that he was not insensible. Greer had refused to answer questions about making Perry gamble with him, the use of foul language to him, refusing to leave his room, and struggling with him. He had also refused to answer if he had ever had any reason to attack Perry, or if he had been ordered under arrest. Esther Major was not a woman with whom Perry had ever consorted and she had no reason to favour him, but she had heard Perry ask Greer to leave Perry's room, and had heard Greer use disgusting language to him. She had heard a scuffle and when she had come up to Perry's room she had found the two officers in a wrestling position. She had confirmed that Greer had used personal violence to, and had assaulted and grossly insulted, Perry.

Perry thought he was entitled, with respect, to observe that the Deputy Judge Advocate's remarks, doubting if any degree of provocation could persuade the fifteen officers of the court that the alleged assault was justified, tended to prejudge the case and were inconsistent with the rules of law and the principles of common justice, for they suggested that no amount of personal violence, no extent of personal abuse, would justify a man in resorting to force to protect himself from injury and insult. Perry admitted that he had struck Greer, but humbly and respectfully submitted to the court that he had been legally justified in doing so. By the law of England, as laid down in *Blackstone's Commentaries,* one was entitled if struck, or assaulted, in one's defence, to strike the offender and plead *son assault demesne,* or that it was the plaintiff's original assault that occasioned it. One could, if dangerously assaulted and for one's own preservation, even wound or maim an adversary. Secondly, even if no dangerous attack had been made upon him, as he had placed Greer under arrest (which he has not denied), by the articles of war his continued attack would have justified still stronger measures than those adopted. Thirdly, that the brutal attack made upon him in his own room, the infamous epithets heaped upon him, Greer's refusal to leave, and the continued personal violence from a man superior in height, weight and strength, would produce excitement and a loss of self control which would excuse Perry's conduct and entitle him to the court's lenient and merciful consideration. Fourthly, he had always conducted himself as a peaceful and quiet man, as becoming an officer and a gentleman, and had always shown kindness and forbearance to his brother officers, so that an isolated act of violence in the heat of an unguarded moment should not be allowed to militate against his character and prospects in life. He hoped that the President and members would look with consideration on the conduct of a young officer, without father, friends or advisers; who had uniformly borne an upright reputation; who had always acted with kindness and never with malevolence towards others; but who, under strong provocation had been induced to commit an act of violence, which however justifiable, he deeply deplored. He left himself in their hands, with the conviction that they would say that he was not guilty of the charge against him.

The Court had listened with deep interest to Perry's statement. The President had objected to no part of it, and it seemed to have produced a favourable impression. Colonel Garrett was invited to make a reply, but said that although there were one or two statements in the defence which he could contradict, they were of general assertions and did not bear upon the point at issue and he would not therefore take up the Court's time by noticing them.

The Court was cleared, and sat in deliberation until half past 2 o'clock when it broke up. The verdict, and any sentence, would not be promulgated until approved by the General Commanding-in-Chief and confirmed by Her Majesty. So ended the newspaper report printed on Saturday, July 15th.

Thunder from *The Times*...

In the same issue, *The Times* commented forcefully in a leading article on the circumstances leading to, and on the trial itself.

The first target was the Deputy Judge Advocate for suggesting that no amount of provocation would justify the assault alleged. The newspaper doubted this. As the facts had been made widely known, those readers who mixed with persons of tidier morals and cleaner minds, should not be shocked by the newspaper's account of such vice and brutality. It was a shame and scandal that scenes such as those described had occurred among officers of the British army. It was disgraceful to themselves and their regiment. An end must be put to such practices, or the name of an officer will certainly cease to be synonymous with that of a gentleman. There was no use hushing such matters up. The greater the publicity, the greater the scandal, and it was only from the extent of the scandal that a remedy can be expected.

The leader described again the events of the night and early morning of the 28th/29th June. It described the language used by Greer to Perry as terms which the most foul-mouthed ruffian in London might perhaps, in a moment of high excitement, have used to a pot-companion with whom he had quarrelled. It noted the discrepancy between the two accounts of the scuffle. Greer, it wrote, had alleged that he had been first struck and rendered insensible, and when he had recovered had been struck again. This is what lawyers call 'hard swearing' for its obvious intention to show that the opponent had struck the swearer when he was in a state of half- sensibility. There was a blow, a pause, insensibility, recovery, a fresh scuffle, a fresh blow, a second recovery and the doctor. Fortunately the woman Esther Major had disposed of this hypothesis, for she had testified that she had heard the shouting and the scuffle, had run upstairs at once to see Greer leaning against the washhandstand, not on the floor and not insensible. The assistant-surgeon had also found Greer confused but not unconscious. The attempt to make the court believe that Perry had in cold blood taken advantage of Greer's insensibility to inflict further injury upon him was simply preposterous, and its vindictiveness reflected very little credit on the accuser whose own conduct, by his own admission, seemed to have been that of a mere ruffian.

Speaking as civilians experienced in criminal courts, the writers had no hesitation in saying that, on the facts of the case, a conviction for common assault could not possibly be obtained. Was there a man in England who would have done less than Perry had? Would not nine men out of ten have done more? The law of England justifies and excuses such acts as his. But the courtmartial would not look just at the law, but would consider whether a gentleman should have acted as Perry did. It was certainly true that Perry should have avoided such bad society, and would have better prepared himself for his regimental duties the next day if he had retired to bed, but it was clear that the custom of this regiment was to partake in such debaucheries and it was unfair to make a lad just out of his teens the victim of so scandalous a system. The public would hardly believe that Colonel Robert Garrett, the Commanding Officer who appeared as prosecutor, was not responsible for the condition of his regiment. He could not exercise constant scrutiny over his subalterns but it was acknowledged that a good commanding officer gave the tone to his regiment. Perry had actually applied to his colonel for protection from the persecution of his brother officers. Was this evidence of barrack life typical of other regiments? Do the younger officers habitually sit up playing cards, at roulette and what not, all night? Do they introduce their mistresses into barracks at their will and pleasure? Can a system of bullying worse than any public school exist where all are supposed to be 'officers and gentlemen'? Can other commanding officers not succeed better than Colonel Garrett? The newspaper hoped that they would do better, and that the public might in future be spared the spectacle of a commanding officer prosecuting a wretched lad who would never have appeared before a court martial if the Colonel had done his duty.

Public reaction – and Greer is also court-martialled

By now the interest of the general public in the case was at fever point. Retired officers and gentlemen all over the country spoke of little else. At the Horse Guards, where the Commander-in-Chief, Lord Hardinge, presided, there was great concern over what would be the court's finding, whether guilty or not, for the army seemed doomed to lose in public eyes whatever was done. The first step, however, seemed clear. The evidence given in the trial had been clear: Lieutenant Greer had acted appallingly towards Perry, and had himself committed offences which ought to be brought to trial. Belatedly, and no doubt after being firmly prompted, Colonel Garrett at last formally reported this, through his superiors, to Horse Guards and a second court martial was ordered - this time on Greer.

Chapter 4 – Greer's Court-Martial

On Friday, July 21st 1854, another court martial assembled at Windsor Barracks. This time the accused was Lieutenant Thomas Fergus Greer and he was charged with Conduct unbecoming an officer and gentleman; and to the prejudice of good order and military discipline, in the following respects: for having, on the night 28/29 June, wilfully struck and offered other personal violence to Lieutenant James Edward Perry, for having at the same time and place used provoking, insulting and disgusting language to Perry, calling him 'swindler', 'blackguard' and using other language of an offensive and insulting nature. Again Colonel Garrett prosecuted, but now Colonel the Hon Arthur Upton, Coldstream Guards, presided. Members of the court were Colonel Charles William Balders (unattached), Lieutenant Colonel the Hon Cecil Forester MP and Lieutenant Colonel H.R.Howard Vyse MP, both of the Royal Horse Guards (Blue), Major Henry Brewster of the 76th, Major S.T.Christie of the 80th, Major G.F.Stevenson Call, 18th, Captain W.Murray, 10th Hussars, Captain F.A.Sykes, 94th, Captains G.D.Pitt and J.Lawrie, 80th, Captain Robert Sheffield, Royal Horse Guards (Blue), Lieutenant A.C.White, 12th Lancers, Lieutenant W.Paterson, 80th, Lieutenant T.Esmonde,18th. The Deputy Judge Advocate was Lieutenant Colonel Pipon. Mr E.Creasy of London, barrister-at-law, instructed by Mr G.H.Long, solicitor of Windsor, attended on the part of the accused.

Greer had no objection to either the President nor the Deputy Judge Advocate, and pleaded 'Not Guilty' to the charge. As in Perry's case, the witnesses first made statements which were recorded by the Deputy Judge Advocate, then the prosecution and defence could put their own questions in writing and submit them to the court, and if approved the President would ask them. Perry and Esther Major were called by the Prosecution, and Assistant-Surgeon Dempster, Surgeon Webb, Major Maxwell, Adjutant M'Alester and Captain Sandwith by the Defence.

Perry's evidence

The remaining witnesses were ordered out of court as Perry was sworn and began his evidence. This was largely as recorded in his own trial, but Perry asked if he could add that he freely forgave Greer and that Greer had expressed regret that he had treated a brother officer as he had. Garrett asked if Greer had been drunk or sober. He was neither drunk nor sober, replied Perry. He could not remember how many times he had struck Greer with the candlesticks. Greer then cross-examined, (in writing, through the court). Perry said that the two had never quarrelled before, but there had been bad feeling between them. He agreed that there had been instances of practical joking among the officers, but denied that he had ever taken part himself, and specifically not against Lieutenant William Waldy. He agreed that while playing billiards the two had occasionally laughed, but Greer had not laughed when he was losing. Perry had not used abusive language himself and was not in the habit of using such language. He had not shown the bruises he claimed to have suffered in the scuffling to anyone as M'Alester, the adjutant, had said he would send Captain Sandwith to see them, and Sandwith had never come. Perry was in arrest and had not been able to go and find Sandwith. Perry had not called out for help from other officers when Greer was alleged to have been attacking him as he did not know if any were there, and in any case he thought that anyone would have heard him and Greer arguing.

Perry is cross-examined

Greer put a series of questions designed to show that Captain Nicholas was in his room nearby and some months earlier, when Lieutenant and Adjutant, had reprimanded young officers who had been ragging Perry. Perry said that he had complained to the colonel, but did not know that Nicholas had spoken to anyone. He thought Nicholas had himself ill-treated new officers on their joining. Greer suggested that both Colonel Garrett and Major Maxwell had intervened on Perry's behalf after complaints. Perry could not remember Major Maxwell ever doing so, and thought Colonel Garrett's intervention, when he had reprimanded an officer in Perry's presence, had been insufficient and merely a matter of 'form'. Twice the room had been cleared while the court considered Greer's line of questioning and finally the Deputy Judge Advocate ruled that it did not bear on the charge. Greer's two final questions brought answers: Perry had not complained to the commanding officer since, though he thought that he had had reason. He did not remember on which temple he had struck Greer, but had not used his full force, and though the blood had flowed, he was certain that Greer had not reeled. The court adjourned at 4 o'clock.

The next day, Saturday 22nd July, Perry's indirect cross-examination was resumed. He could not remember how many blows he had struck. Greer's next question was lengthy: 'You have stated that I called you "poor", and that you played against your wish so long that night, have you not, while in the regiment, been frequently engaged in play?' Perry said not more than two or three times. The President said that he had not answered fully. 'It is so long', said Perry, 'it is more like a sermon than a question'.

57

Colonel Pipon, the Deputy Judge Advocate, interjected: 'It is!' Perry asked what was meant by play, and the President said billiards, cards, or anything. Surely Perry knew what play was? He asked if play for money was meant. Certainly, said the President. Then no, said Perry, I have not repeatedly played for money, not more than twice. Greer now put to him certain specific instances. Had he not gambled for money at the game of French hazard, or green cloth, at the Three Tuns. Perry admitted that he had, but only at Greer's earnest request. He denied that he had gambled at Cork, for he had only played billiards there, with a civilian friend, for small points. Greer's next question was refused by the court after all members had studied it, and the President advised Perry that he need not answer any question that did not bear strictly on the charge. Perry said he had no objection to any question, but Greer had finished.

When the Deputy Judge Advocate read over his testimony, Perry sought to amend his earlier answer on the proximity to his own of Captain Nicholas's room, for he had now ascertained that it was two storeys below his own, not one, and Captain Nicholas would not have heard Perry cry for help unless he had gone to the top of the stairs. This and another amendment, the court did not think material, but they made the corrections that Perry asked for.

Re-examination of Perry

Colonel Garrett, the Prosecutor, now asked more questions in re-examination. Perry said that the scuffles had all taken place in the Infantry Barracks, Windsor. He and Greer had not returned to the barracks together after playing billiards. In the billiard room Greer had at first won six shillings, but by tossing double or quits this had become a loss to Greer of five pounds. He had been in plain clothes. He had gone to Greer's room only when asked to go, in the anteroom, to drink some wine and see Greer's woman.

Captain O'Toole had also been in the anteroom. Perry was not in the habit of going to Greer's room to gamble, and had only been there three times in his life, and never before to play. He had not expected to have to play, and had gone for a drink of wine. Colonel Forester asked if Perry or Greer had first proposed the game at billiards. Perry thought he had already answered this. He paused, and then said that he had no objection to saying that he had proposed it. A member of the court, Captain Pitt, intervened to protest at this answer being recorded. He had not sought to play, he had been the only person left in the room and had played only to gratify Greer. He could not be said to have suggested the game; there was a marked difference between the two statements.

Perry was pressed over his statement that Greer had been neither drunk, nor sober. Was he fit for duty? Perry said that Greer always seemed half-drunk, but he had seen him on duty in a worse condition. He thought that he knew what he was about, but could not precisely say whether he was fit for duty or not.

'Greer's woman' testifies

Esther Major, a girl about 19 years old, was then called and sworn. She said much of what she had said in the Perry court-martial. Greer had persuaded a reluctant Perry to gamble and had used bad language when he had been losing. Perry had twice gone back to his own room, and the first time Greer had brought him back, holding his coat, but with both officers laughing. The second time, Greer had followed him and she had at first heard laughter, but then their voices became angry and she had heard a scuffle. She had run upstairs to Perry's room and seen Greer leaning against the washhand-stand, his face streaming with blood. She had been alarmed and had run away. She had not seen any violence from, or blows struck by Greer, and she had not seen him push Perry down on a chair in his room. She had heard him insulting Perry and calling him a '----' and a 'son of a -----' but she had not heard him say 'swindler' nor 'blackguard'. She had not thought Greer tipsy though he was rather excited by drink. She did not think Perry was drunk, though he had taken wine and, pressed by Greer, she agreed that Perry had also said to him 'be -- ----- to Hell'.

Greer's Defence

Greer began his defence by calling the Assistant Surgeon, Dempster. He repeated the evidence he had given at Perry's court-martial. He had counted seven wounds on Greer's scalp, and had found two more later. Two of the wounds were serious, but he could not say how much force had been used in causing them. He did not think that any degree of insensibility would have resulted. He had seen no marks of violence on Perry.

The court then adjourned until Monday 24 July when Greer called his second and final witness, Major Maxwell[44] of the

---

[44] Maxwell's 'robust attitude' to rough horseplay, even as far as incidents involving civilians which exhibited a lack of commonsense, decency and good manners, had been revealed when he was a subaltern in March 1844 and stationed in Gibraltar. He had been in a brawl which followed when a party of officers, including him, clashed with civilian shop-keepers who objected to them vandalising their wares. Maxwell came off worst but was rescued by a British sentry who took him and his assailant to the guard room. Next day the civilian was tried in the civil court for his part in the affair but was acquitted and promptly sued Maxwell for assault and false imprisonment. Despite four brother officers testifying to his innocence, the court found against him and Maxwell was ordered to pay £100 for the assault, and another

regiment. Maxwell had known Greer for the five years he had been in the regiment, and thought that he had lived on terms of intimacy and friendship with his brother officers. He had never known him to be drunk, or unfitted by drinking, when on duty. Maxwell had reprimanded, in Perry's presence, officers about whom Perry had complained. He had also been present when Colonel Garrett, in Perry's presence, had reprimanded an officer about whom Perry had complained and that reprimand had been as formal and severe as it could have been. Colonel Garrett then asked supplementary questions on the subject of this same reprimand. Maxwell agreed that the colonel had forbidden the officer in question to enter Perry's room at any time of day or night, and thought that all annoyance to Perry had ceased at that time. The court asked Maxwell if Captain Nicholas had been in the habit of ill-treating officers, especially young officers on first joining the regiment. Maxwell said that he had never heard it, and thought Nicholas one of the kindest officers in the regiment, especially towards young officers. The court asked if Maxwell meant to say that Nicholas had never been in the habit of playing practical jokes on young officers on joining. Maxwell replied 'I do not' and after a pause added 'To the best of my knowledge'.

Greer asked for two-hours to prepare his final statement and the Court adjourned until 2 p.m.

Perry's letter to the Court

When it reassembled, Perry handed in a letter, which was later to have a dramatic effect. The letter was not entered in the court minutes, and a Mr Bullock then addressed the court-martial. He explained that he was not Greer's professional adviser, but was related to him by marriage. He read out Greer's statement.

£100 for false imprisonment - huge sums in those days. The Court-Martial was, of course, unaware of this.

Greer's Defence Statement

After the usual courtesies, Greer pointed out that he had had to defend himself from accusations which placed in jeopardy his fortune, character and all prospects in life, and he had already been attacked by the most powerful organs of public opinion and prejudged by all the world before he could defend himself. He had been held up as a convicted ruffian and the press had employed its highest power of invective to make him an object of public notice and public hatred wherever the English language was known. He had been anxious to defend the case, not just for his own sake, but also for his regiment. His brother-officers had been attacked, and the credit of his regiment had been injured. It was a regiment in which he had always met with friendship and kindness. In it he had passed five happy years, and he had hoped, and still hoped, to pass many more. Whatever his fate, it was a regiment whose honour would ever be as dear to him as his own.

There were two charges against him, one of blows and one of words. He would be as brief as possible, and he would not impute to Lieutenant Perry the crime of having deliberately invented a string of perjuries for the purpose of ruining him for he would be sorry to believe that of anyone, let alone one holding Her Majesty's Commission. He did not wish to defend himself by heaping cruel charges on another, even if he had been shown no forbearance in that respect. He would not follow a bad example.

But he must ask the court to consider the peculiar circumstances in which Perry gave evidence against him. There were the strongest inducements on any human to colour the events as much as possible against an accused person. Self-interest and self-preservation would lead to events which were favourable to the accuser being recalled, while those favourable to the accused were forgotten. This was especially so if the scene which the

62

witness tried to recollect was one of drink and high play, boisterous jocularity, loss of temper and serious violence. A man's memory in such cases was not to be trusted, and it was hard when the accused was not himself allowed to give evidence. The court should look for corroboration of what the witness said, and only in one respect was that found in this case, on a matter to which Greer would return.

Meanwhile he asked the court to remember the witness's demeanour and how in his evidence he had pressed hard against Greer even on matters that were not relevant to the charges. For example, when asked if Greer had been fit for duty, Perry might well have answered directly yes or no, or have said that he could not answer. Instead Perry had immediately begun to offer a number of assertions that he had seen Greer more drunk while on duty, and that it was well-known that he was often drunk on duty. The court had checked Perry when he had tried to give those answers and had disregarded them, but the spirit of ill-will which had prompted them was self-evident. Major Maxwell's evidence had refuted such allegations of habitual drunkenness, but the court should remember them when considering whether they were bound to convict Greer on Perry's testimony against him.

Greer did not pretend that he was entirely innocent and the injured party with regard to the events of the night of 28th June. He would always feel regret and shame in thinking of those events. But many a man had served his country through long years of maturer age with honour and esteem, both in military and social life, who would have been a ruined outcast if some foolish prank or culpable excess at the age of 25 had been dealt with as a grave breach of his duty as an officer and a gentleman. He earnestly hoped that a calm review of his case would permit a lenient judgement which would not compromise discipline or represent a failure of justice. He reviewed the facts of the case against him which he thought were beyond dispute, but stressed how Perry had sought to colour the facts, and had denied at first, until cross-examined, that there had been laughter from both officers throughout the early incidents. Esther Major had confirmed this, and though she had said that he used offensive language to Perry she had been in a different room for much of the time and might easily have mistaken the words being used. For instance, the words 'poor beggar' pronounced in a hasty conversation might have sounded from afar like a word of nearly similar sound, but infinitely more loathsome. As far as the events in Perry's room were concerned, why had Perry not secured the door if he had feared that Greer was bothering him? And why, in an occupied building, had he not cried out for help, rather than assault his alleged attacker? Why was no evidence found of Perry being bruised if he had been attacked as he claimed? Perry's evidence on other points had also been refuted by other witnesses. He had said that Captain Nicholas was in the habit of ill-treating young officers upon joining. He had asserted that Major Maxwell had never reprimanded anyone against whom he had complained. He had said that Colonel Garrett had administered only a slight reprimand, a mere matter of form, and quite insufficient in Perry's opinion. All of these statements had been disproved by evidence given by others. Finally he had sought to give the impression that the candlestick broken in the assault had been loose in its socket before, and had not broken because of the violence of the attack. Greer thought that examination of the candlesticks, bloodstained and dented, and Greer's wounds, showed the violence of the blows struck.

Greer thanked the Court for their patience, and confident in their fairness hoped that they would think his bodily and mental suffering were sufficient punishment for any degree of blame which attached to him for the transaction. He hoped that their verdict would not consign him to utter ruin, and bring further misery on all with whom he was connected.

The court was cleared, and the members deliberated. The sentence would not be promulgated until it had been confirmed by highest authority.

Newspaper comment

The Times returned to the subject of the two court-martials in the next issue's leader columns. It expressed itself indifferent to the fate of Greer: whether or not it was right for him to continue to hold the Queen's commission was not its concern. But Perry's case was very different. He had been arraigned for doing what any young man with a spark of manly feeling would have done on less provocation. He had been subjected to a long course of bullying; he had been abused; he was bespattered with the most foul and obscene epithets; he had been attacked by a man of superior strength; and at last indignation had got the better of his indecision and he had seized a candlestick from a nearby table and knocked down his assailant. Who among its readers would have done less? Lord Hardinge, a man of untarnished honour, a soldier of courage, bright and polished as his sword, was at the head of the army. Even now that age had in some measure checked the impetuous soldier of Albuhera, what would he have done had he been selected by a vulgar bully as the object of insult so intolerable? What would he have done but what Lieutenant Perry did? Perry, this unlucky lad, would have done better to keep out of bad company, that is, to have nothing to do with his brother officer. Greer's defence did not shake one single fact advanced by Perry, confirmed where necessary by unwilling witnesses. It was surprising to find the bully bringing the charge of 'vindictiveness' against his victim. Greer in the earlier case had tried to give the impression that Perry had attacked him more than once, while he was in a state of half-insensibility. And he had repeatedly refused to answer questions which Perry thought it necessary to put to him. There was no conceivable question which he should have refused to answer. Here was poor Perry fighting his battle with every man's hand against him; the Colonel of his regiment the accuser, and interposing at every moment with any suggestion which might damnify his case; the Deputy Judge Advocate pulling him up whenever there was an opportunity and pretending to be the friend of both sides, while he was in reality pressing against one. Every man against him, but Perry had the wit and courage to defend himself in a manner which will not speedily be forgotten. The public will not readily believe that colonel Garrett, the commanding officer, is not most deeply to blame for the condition in which his regiment is found to be.

Chapter 5 - A second Court-martial for Perry!

The next day, Saturday 29th July, *The Times* contained a brief, but astonishing announcement. There was to be a second courtmartial of Lieutenant Perry! A court had assembled at Windsor on the Thursday when an order from the Commander-in-Chief, under the Royal sign manual, had been read, for the trial, but without specifying the charges. The warrants appointing the President and Deputy Judge Advocate were also read. The court had then adjourned until the Saturday. Lieutenant Perry had not been present, but his legal adviser, Mr Darvill, the Town Clerk of Windsor was, and had pressed for details of the charges against Perry. The Deputy Judge Advocate had courteously declined, and it was understood that he himself did not know at that time. Darvill pointed out that under the sixth section of the Mutiny Act a court had to be summoned to try a specific offence. This was like trying a man under a General Warrant, which would allow all sorts of accusations to be raked up against him. The Deputy Judge Advocate said that he could not discuss such matters, but Lieutenant Perry could rest assured that due notice would be given him of any charge which was preferred.

The paper commented that it was the general opinion of the public that Perry was being tried for the third time for his one offence, even before the verdict of the first trial had been given. By the mode of cross-examination allowed at the second trial, he was virtually tried a second time, and in that trial it had appeared that Colonel Garrett had been the prosecutor against him, not against Lieutenant Greer, whom he had but nominally proceeded against.

On the Saturday, the court assembled, again at Windsor, with Colonel Thomas Edward Kelly of the Provisional Battalion as President, and the following twelve members: Lieutenant Colonels Parker, 1st Life Guards; Spencer Percival, Coldstream Guards; Fosdyce, 13th Foot; Forester, Grenadier Guards, and AF Blyth of the Cavalry Depot; Captains E.W.D. Lowe, 32nd Regiment; C.Sawyer, 6th Dragoon Guards; the Earl of Longford, 2nd Life Guards; W.H.C.G. Pochell, 77th Regiment; R.G. Ainslie, 1st Dragoon Guards; J. Howard-Vyse, Royal Horse Guards (Blue); and H. Mackay, 79th Highlanders; and Lieutenants O.M. Priam, 94th Regiment and R.G. Brady, 1st Royal Regiment of Foot. The members were sworn, Perry not objecting to any of them. Major J.W.Dalgetty[45] officiated as Deputy Judge Advocate, and General Wetherall, the Deputy Adjutant General of the Forces, was in attendance, it is presumed as prosecutor. Colonel Upton, President at Greer's Courtmartial, and Lieutenant Colonel Pipon, Deputy Judge Advocate at that same trial, were present as witnesses. Nearly all the officers of the 46th were also in the room.

Perry, attended by Mr Darvill, listened intently as the charges were read, to a gasp from the room, for they appeared to

---

[45] Dalgety was the Brigade Major at Portsmouth and unattached to a regiment. He appears to have lacked confidence in his judicial role and there were several exchanges of letters between him and the Deputy Judge Advocate General as he sought advice from the latter. On one occasion he forwarded a portion of the record of proceedings seeking approval, and was reminded that it was not usual to send such portions, but only the complete record when the proceedings were concluded. See WO 81/99.

observers quite unprecedented. He was charged with scandalous, infamous conduct, unbecoming an Officer and a Gentleman, in the following instances:

First, for having in a certain letter, dated Windsor Barracks, July 24th, 1854, and addressed to Colonel the Honourable Arthur Upton, President of the General Court martial then and there assembled for the trial of Lieutenant T.F. Greer, which letter bore the signature of the prisoner, and was then and there delivered to the said Colonel Upton - made the following slanderous statement respecting his commanding officer, Lieutenant Colonel Garrett, viz:- 'that after repeated acts of violence against myself (meaning the prisoner) (by other officers of the 46th while the regiment was in Dublin) in my Bedroom, I reported the circumstances to Colonel Garrett, who reproached me and called me a fool for my pains;' he the said prisoner then well knowing that so much of the said statement as relates to Lieutenant Colonel Garrett, viz: the words 'who reproached me and called me a fool for my pains,' was false.

The remaining three charges may be paraphrased as follows. Second, another charge relating to the same letter, in so far as he had said that until he had threatened to appeal to the General of the district, and had written to Colonel Garrett saying so, no action had been taken by the colonel in respect of the bullying to which he had been subjected. The charge stated that he had never threatened the colonel, either by word of mouth or in writing and to claim so was false.

Third, for having in the Greer trial said that Captain Nicholas had himself ill-treated other officers on joining, when this was false.

Fourth, for having written to the Deputy Judge Advocate stating that Major Maxwell's evidence to the court that Nicholas had never ill-treated young officers was wrong and he could prove it, when that was false.

The charges were noted as 'By Order of the General Commanding-in-Chief, G.A.Wetherall, DAG (Deputy Adjutant General)'.

The Deputy Judge Advocate explained to Perry that the court wished to give him every possible facility in his defence, and would allow time before he pleaded if he wished. Perry said he would now plead 'Not Guilty' but he would like to ask for time to prepare his defence. The President asked when the prisoner had received the charges and was told that they had been delivered to him only that morning. Several members of the court spoke out to say that that was unusually short notice and that he ought to have time allowed to him. Perry addressed the court, and said that he would be ready to proceed as soon as his witnesses were ready. He would hand in a list of them, but it would be some time before they could attend. Meanwhile he wondered if he might be placed on parole, as the room in which he was confined was only twelve feet by ten feet, and though not injurious to his health was depressing to his spirit. He had been there for thirty-one days already. He was confident that he would be found not guilty of the new charges, and this continuous imprisonment would be a punishment as undeserved as it was painful. How much time do you need, asked the President? I cannot say when the witnesses will be ready, replied Perry, as some of them are in Turkey, and other parts. I thought as much, said the President and there was laughter in court. The public were cleared from the court and readmitted half an hour later.

The President then told Perry that he would be given any reasonable time, but would have to apply for this at the proper time. It could not comment on his state of arrest as that was a mere matter of discipline for his commanding officer. Colonel Garrett asked if he might address the court on this, and was told firmly that he could not: the court had made its position clear. Perry then said that on one or two occasions Colonel Garrett had kindly given him leave to go and see Mr Darvill, for which he begged to thank him

The Deputy Judge Advocate then pressed him as to how much time he would need to prepare his defence. Perry asked if he could have his witnesses? He was told that at this stage all that he was being asked was how much time he needed. He asked for until a week on Monday - just over a week. The Deputy Judge Advocate thought this unreasonable: twenty-four hours was normal. Then until next Thursday, asked Perry. The charges were so numerous that they needed consideration. He was told that he would only need to listen to the evidence, not to start on his defence. Then how much can I have, said Perry. The President then ruled until Monday - effectively no extra time at all. Perry then asked for a copy of the minutes of Greer's trial. The Deputy Judge Advocate said that this was out of the power of the court as the court could not even have them itself. Perry then handed in the following remarks: It was contrary to the law of evidence to enter upon charges based on evidence given by him in the trial of Lieutenant Greer without the production of the original minutes of that evidence as those minutes were the best and only evidence of what was stated, and he submitted that he should be furnished with extracts of such minutes as far as they affected the charges against him.

The President thought that all the evidence had been published, but Perry thought that what had been published had differed materially from the minutes. The Deputy Judge Advocate said that the Judge Advocate was the custodier of the minutes, and Perry had better apply to him. Finally, Perry tried unsuccessfully to direct attention to a clause in the Mutiny Act, and the Court adjourned until the Monday.

71

Newspaper comment

Led by *The Times,* newspapers and magazines now poured forth indignation! In a powerful leader, the 'Thunderer' wrote on the Tuesday, as follows: We supposed that after having recorded our opinion on the two Courts-martial held at Windsor we had entirely done with the subject, unless, indeed it might be necessary to refer to it when the finding and sentence should be made known. We were, however, it seems, entirely mistaken. It has been thought fit, a second time to subject Mr Perry to trial, the charge on this occasion arising from certain statements made by Lieutenant Perry in his former trial and in that of Mr Greer, in which he was examined nominally as a witness, but in which he was almost as much a defendant as in the case which bears his own name. When we consider the nature of the first charge against Lieutenant Perry, and remember that from that time to the present he has with the exception of a few visits to his legal adviser, been kept a close prisoner, we must consider the proceedings against this young officer as deeply stained with harshness and injustice. The opinion of the public has already anticipated the tardy justice of the Court-martial [not yet made public], and has pronounced in the first case a verdict of triumphal acquittal. No blame attaches to the authorities for directing such an inquiry. The great injury sustained by one officer at the hands of another naturally demanded investigation, and that investigation necessarily took the form of a charge against Lieutenant Perry. His vindication was, however, so complete that we feel quite sure no judge or jury in this country could have come to any other conclusion than that his assault upon Mr Greer, violent as it was, was more than justified by the provocation, and the authorities ought therefore to have felt that the necessary inquiry had inflicted on Mr Perry much undeserved suffering, and thrown upon an innocent man the burden of probing that guilt for which his accusers ought in the first instance to have been called upon to answer. Under these circumstances the clear duty of the military authorities was to terminate the unjust persecution of Lieutenant Perry as soon as possible, to restore him to his liberty, and to take immediate and effectual measures for eradicating the spirit of tyranny among subordinates, and laxity among chiefs, for which the 46th Regiment has become so unhappily remarkable. Had Mr Greer and Mr Perry been civilians, a preliminary investigation before magistrates would have done justice to the merits of the case, and relieved Mr Perry from the necessity of going any further into the circumstances of an assault which the bare recital of the facts so completely justifies.

Necessity excused the first trial, but where shall we find the palliation for the second? In which of the darkest periods of history shall we search in order to find the parallel for accusing a man of an offence of which he proves himself entirely innocent, and then treating the statements he puts forth in his expiation as libels on which to ground a series of fresh accusations? This is a refinement of oppression to which even Scroggs or Jeffries never aspired. Popham, on the trial of Sir Walter Raleigh, bade him 'be valiant for his life'; and the worst of our judges, however ready to catch at the unguarded admission of the prisoner, never thought of making his statements the grounds of fresh charges against him. The charges against Lieutenant Perry did not, it is true, point specifically to matters alleged by him on his own trial but the subterfuge is merely technical. Lieutenant Perry had been tried for assaulting Lieutenant Greer; Lieutenant Greer was then tried for assaulting and abusing Lieutenant Perry. The finding and sentence on Lieutenant Perry were still unknown, and he was, as we have remarked, still virtually, though not technically, on his defence. Being contradicted on Mr Greer's trial by witnesses whom he had not had the opportunity of cross-examining, and from whom the prosecutor was not disposed to protect him, Mr Perry took the course, neither unusual nor improper, of addressing a letter to the

President of the Court-martial, explaining away and refuting the statements of the witnesses. This was nothing more than making a supplemental defence to a supplemental accusation. If ever a communication was privileged surely such a letter, the effort of a man under accusation to clear himself from additional charges by the only means in his power, ought to have been considered so; but the justice which is extended to the meanest criminal is denied to officers and gentlemen, and we are shocked with the spectacle of a young man first made the victim of a most cruel and unmanly outrage, then put upon his trial for a mere act of self-defence, and then reaccused because those whom his defence criminates will not subscribe to the truth of his censures! How could it be known that the statements contained in Mr Perry's letter and evidence were infamous, scandalous and false? Every probablility is in favour of their truth. It is not improbable, considering the infamous treatment to which young officers in the 46th were undoubtedly subject, that captains had assisted and colonels connived at it, nor that the victim, driven to desperation, should have threatened an appeal to the General of the district. Where such things take place the commanding officer is sure to be in fault; and the very injustice with which Mr Perry is now persecuted shows how little he had to hope from the men whose position constituted them his natural protectors. If there was to be a second investigation, and we are far from denying its justice, the prisoner ought to have been, not Lieutenant Perry, but the Colonel commanding the regiment, and a man once wrongfully accused ought not to have been a second time subjected to a contest in which all the power that rank, influence, and position place at the disposal of the commanding officer was sure to be employed against him. The proceedings are of a piece with their institution. The court met on Saturday last at half-past 11 o'clock to enter on the consideration of a charge which had only been delivered to the accused that morning. Major Maxwell and Captain Nicholas, two of the principal witnesses to be called against Mr Perry, were most improperly allowed to be present. His statement that some of the witnesses he wished to call were in Turkey was received by the Court with a laugh and a jocular remark that they 'thought so!' The third and fourth charges were based on the evidence given by Mr Perry on the trial of Mr Greer. He most reasonably applied for the minutes of that evidence. The application was refused, and he was referred to the newspaper reports. At last he obtained an adjournment of the case from Saturday till Monday, - 48 hours, as he was consolingly reminded. We would advise the military authorities, both central and local, to cut short as speedily as possible this degrading persecution, and to remember that in the eyes of an impartial public the judges and the prosecutor are quite as much on their trial as the prisoner.

The third day

Another surprise awaited the court when it resumed on the Monday, 31st July. The prosecutor was to be Major General Wetherall, Deputy-Adjutant-General of the Forces, from the Commander-in-Chief's headquarters at Horse Guards. Meanwhile Mr Darvill, Perry's legal adviser, was not present. General Wetherall explained that he was there at the direct wish of the Commander- in-Chief, Viscount Hardinge, and that the court had been convened, not only to give the accused an opportunity of substantiating the complaints he had made by cross-examining the officers of his regiment, or any other means, but also to give Colonel Garrett and other officers of the regiment the chance to answer those complaints by answering on oath in open court, questions from the prosecutor, prisoner or court. The ends of justice and the discovery of truth could be better attained by this court than by a Court of Inquiry, which would not hear evidence on oath, could not compel civilian witnesses to attend, and would be, by service custom, a closed court. Lord Hardinge had therefore ordered the Court-martial in justice to Lieutenant Perry and the officers of the regiment, and also for the maintenance of good conduct and gentlemanly behaviour among all officers of Her Majesty's army. He asked the court to allow the prisoner as much indulgence as was consistent with regular procedure, and to enter the inquiry with open minds, entirely free from prejudice one way or the other. There should be no vindictiveness against the prisoner. He felt also compelled to say that Colonel Garrett and the other officers concerned were most anxious to have a full inquiry into the various matters alleged against them.

He outlined the case against Perry. The first and second charges were of making false statements against Colonel Garrett. Perry had sent a letter to the President of the Court- martial on Greer, alleging acts of grave injustice, and that Garrett had been kept in the path of duty only by threats of exposure. The letter was not in Perry's handwriting, but it bore his signature. All the officers of the regiment, except those already embarked for the East - Captains O'Toole and Hardy, Lieutenants Shervinton and Knapp, and Ensigns Helyer and Townshend - would give evidence. The third and fourth charges related to allegations against Captain Nicholas.

The witnesses all withdrew, but for the regiment's Orderly Sergeant, James Hampson, who told how during Greer's trial he had delivered a letter to Colonel Upton, the president. It had been from a civilian gentleman he did not know, but whom he had seen sitting in the court. Perry had not been present. Colonel Upton then identified the letter and confirmed that he had received it. It was read to the court.

'Sir, It has been communicated to me that since I gave evidence Major Maxwell has been called by Lieutenant Greer, rather to impeach the truth of my evidence than to speak to any substantive part of the present charge; and I beg most respectfully, as I can expect no support from the prosecutor to submit to your hon. Court that if I had been permitted , in my own defence and in vindication of my word and truthfulness, to have cross-examined Major Maxwell, I should have been in a situation to bring to his recollection circumstances upon which he appears to be unfortunately oblivious. I may further submit that the addition that I on Saturday was anxious to have made to my evidence would have brought to light the following facts:- First, that after repeated acts of violence by other officers of the 46th, while the regiment was quartered in Dublin, I reported the circumstances to Colonel Garrett, who reproached me and called me a fool for my pains. Secondly I then patiently submitted to a series of similar indignities, when I complained to Major Maxwell, who represented the facts to Colonel Garrett, upon which he gave the offenders a reprimand. So weak was the effect of the reprimand or caution given by Colonel Garrett that, though the acts of aggression were discontinued, yet I was persecuted in other ways, until I threatened to appeal to the general of the district, and sent a letter to that effect to Colonel Garrett. I was earnestly entreated by several of my brother officers to forebear making any complaint. I did forebear, and from that time I was relieved from any repetition of the annoyances and indignities under which I had formerly laboured. I may also add, that I am prepared to substantiate by evidence all that I have stated with regard to Captain Nicholas; and I place myself in the hands of the Court to do justice to me, because I find that the questions, or similar ones, which I sought to put when on my trial, and which were rejected, have been put without objection before the present court- martial. Of this course I do not complain, but, as far as the court-martial by which I was tried is concerned, I do most seriously complain, inasmuch as I was necessarily prevented from procuring from adverse witnesses the evidence essential to my defence. Trusting that my painful position will be received as my excuse for thus troubling you, I have the honour to be, Sir,

77

Your most obedient humble servant,
J.E. Perry
Windsor Barracks, July 24'

Colour Sergeant John Ellis and Corporal John Smith were called in turn and gave evidence that they were familiar with Perry's signature, and the one on the letter seemed to be his, although the letter itself was in different handwriting. Lieutenant and Adjutant Charles Somerville M'Alester agreed.

Garrett's Evidence

Colonel Robert Garrett was then called and sworn. He did not recollect Perry ever complaining of repeated acts of violence from other officers of the regiment. He had complained however. The first instance which Garrett recalled was at the Linen-hall Barracks in Dublin. While the colonel was sitting with a number of guests in the anteroom he had received a private note from Perry - a hurried, hasty note, complaining that officers were then, or had just been, annoying him in his room. Garrett had asked Major Maxwell to go and see what the trouble was, or to send the adjutant. Maxwell had sent the acting adjutant, who had reported shortly afterwards that the matter was settled. Garrett did not recall what the substance of the complaint was. He had not reproached Perry for complaining, and had not called him 'a fool for his pains'. Nor had he, on that occasion, reprimanded any officer for annoying Perry.

Perry now put in several questions. Garrett thought that Perry had complained to himself or to Major Maxwell on three occasions. He did not know if he had complained to other officers. He agreed that it was the duty of a senior officer to take note of complaints from junior officers if they were sufficiently grave. He agreed that Perry being pulled out of bed nearly every night, his shirt being pulled off his back, and being beaten with an umbrella, was grave enough to be noted. Perry asked if his being made to get into his tub by a number of officers and in their presence to be laughed at, to have his door burst in though he and his servant tried to hold it shut, was this not a proper matter to be reported by senior officers to the colonel? Garrett said that it was most important to prevent ill-will amongst officers to leave something to the discretion of intermediate officers to settle without reference to the commanding officer. At this point Mr Darvill, Perry's solicitor arrived.

Garrett denied that he had called Perry a d----d fool for bothering him, and like a child just escaped from his mother's apron strings, when he had complained of treatment from Curtis and others. He could not recall making any observation to him in the presence of Curtis, Escott, and the then adjutant Sandwith. Pressed by Perry he swore this 'as positively as a man's recollection can go'. His firm conviction was that he had not.

The court was cleared for twenty minutes, and the President then announced that Perry's last question would not be allowed. Perry said that to save the time of the Court he would like to put in a statement. Again the court was cleared of public and the President ruled that the statement was inadmissible. Perry's cross-examination of Garrett resumed.

The colonel declined to say if other officers had been reproached after complaining about being pulled out of their beds as it was not relevant to the case before the court. He had not called Perry 'the malefactor' but had heard the term used, not necessarily about Perry but possibly another officer who had left the regiment. He did not think Perry had been shunned by his brother officers, but he had not been on such intimate terms with the rest of the officers as others. But he had not been under

Garrett's command since December when he had been sent on detachment. Specifically, he had not called Perry a malefactor in front of Lieutenant Knapp. He did not agree that Perry had been 'sent to Coventry' for complaining. If he had been avoided and shunned, and he had no knowledge of such, it was not because he had complained. It must have been because the officers did not like him. Garrett had not kept Perry's note complaining of being annoyed. He had not made any comment on the note. The court adjourned for the day, and reassembled on Tuesday, 1st August when Garrett's cross-examination was resumed.

Garrett remembers little

Garrett could not clearly recall the three occasions when Perry had complained. He thought two were about annoyance in the barrack-room. What the other was he could not say. He thought it was about some dispute. He had not known that on the first occasion, when Perry had sent a note, that Perry had been dragged from his bed, nor had he known that Perry had dressed and had tried to enter the anteroom but had been prevented by two officers, one of whom had threatened to knock him down, and the other who had told him not to be an ass and to go to bed. He had never heard the slightest hint of this.

Garrett was even more vague about the second complaint which had been addressed to Major Maxwell. He had not heard that Perry had written that he could not be expected to get up at 6 o'clock in the morning for drill if his rest was disturbed and every night he was compelled to get out of bed. He thought that Major Maxwell had settled the matter. He did not recollect, nor had the acting adjutant told him, that Perry had threatened to report the circumstances to the general of the Dublin district.

A member of the court, Captain the Earl of Longford, objected to Perry's next question and the court was cleared. On resumption, the prosecutor Major General Wetherall pointed out that for the time being he was restricting himself to the first charge. The court was cleared again, and the President then ruled that the prisoner should do the same, but would be able to recall Colonel Garrett later. Perry argued that he wished to shake the testimony of the witness on the first charge, and his questions were to that end. He sought to show that if Colonel Garrett could not recollect the particulars of the charges then it cannot be said that his statements were false. If the witness was not right upon one point, then how can he be right upon another? The court consulted again, and the Deputy Judge Advocate ruled that Perry's cross-examination should not be restricted to particular charges. Perry asked if the question could now be put and Garrett was asked if Perry had not communicated to him his threat to report the circumstances to the general of the district? Garrett did not recollect anything of the kind.

The court now asked about the later complaints. Garrett said that when he had found that the desired object of stopping annoyance to Perry had not been achieved he had assembled all the junior officers, he thought all the subalterns, and in front of Major Maxwell, the adjutant and Perry himself, had desired that the annoyance should cease, and had reprimanded in particular one officer of whom Perry had specially complained. That officer had been forbidden to enter Perry's room without the colonel's permission. He thought that this had had the desired effect. Garrett thought that a complaint might have reached him about Perry being pulled out of bed while quartered in Dublin, but he could not recollect any details of having his shirt torn, or having been beaten with an umbrella, and he thought it hardly possible that he could have failed to remember such details. Perry had given no reason to suppose that he was not satisfied with the way the complaint had been dealt with. He could recall no further complaints. Perry asked if all the officers had been assembled. Were there more than four? Garrett thought that there were. There were numerous duties, and some officers on leave. He had not paid particular attention to how many officers were present.

Perry asked how, if all annoyance had stopped, Lieutenant Dunscombe had been brought down in his shirt between 1 and 2 o'clock in the morning, in the colonel's presence? Garrett described how one evening he had heard a great deal of noise outside the anteroom where some officers were playing whist. There was a sudden rush of youngsters into the room with Lieutenant Dunscombe who was brought to the door of the anteroom. When he had looked round they all turned and ran away. He supposed that they had not realized that he was there. The President said that Dunscombe had nothing to do with the question before the court. Perry said that he might be a champion for others who had suffered in a like manner to himself. The Deputy Judge Advocate said that Perry could not appear as a champion of others. He had nothing to do with others. Perry had no more questions and Colonel Garrett stood down.

Maxwell testifies

Major Maxwell was the next witness. He remembered the first complaint from Perry. Lieutenant Nicholas, who was then acting as adjutant, had gone to Perry's room and on return to the mess-room had reported to Garrett and Maxwell that all was settled. There had been no inquiry into Perry's complaint. Maxwell was present when the colonel had reprimanded an officer for annoying Perry. He had never heard the colonel reproach Perry for complaining or call him a fool for his pains. He thought there had been three complaints by Perry within two months. The first had been settled by Lieutenant Nicholas. The second had been a written complaint about the conduct of two officers the previous night. Maxwell explained that he had been deputed by the colonel to settle any disputes between junior officers. He had investigated the second complaint and considered that the two officers had behaved improperly towards Perry. At the same time he thought that Perry had given them just cause to complain against him. All three had wanted him to settle the matter without involving the colonel. He had reproved the two officers most severely and had also desired Perry to be more cautious in his conduct. He had also pointed out the impropriety of the note to Colonel Garrett. It had been a very irregular way to lay such a complaint before the commanding officer. Perry had replied that being young in the service he had not known what course to pursue. Maxwell had told him to complain in the first instance to the captain of his company and if the captain could not settle the matter he would send Perry to Maxwell. If it was too serious for Maxwell to deal with it, then he would refer it to the colonel.

He could not remember how the third complaint was made, but was present in the orderly room when the colonel adjudicated on it. Perry stated his grievances against one, or possibly more - he could not remember - officers who were present in plain clothes with the adjutant. The colonel had told the officers how irregular and improper the proceedings were. He then reprimanded the officer most severely and ordered him never to go near Perry's room, by day or night.

Perry asked for details of the cause he had given for complaint in Dublin, to which the major had referred. Maxwell said that Perry had told people in Dublin that one of the officers in question was known in the regiment by a very ugly name. This had given great offence to that officer. Maxwell had therefore judged that there were faults on both sides. Perry said that the question had not been fully answered but the court decided that it had. Perry said that the ugly name mentioned was the *soubriquet* of the officer concerned, and that Maxwell knew this. He had asked Lieutenant Knapp in Maxwell's presence, and Knapp had said so. Maxwell had no recollection of this, and would not have believed it. Perry asked if he could call the officer said to bear the *soubriquet*. General Wetherall thought this would be unusual and the President said he could be called in Perry's defence.

Maxwell did not recall ever receiving a letter from Perry saying that if he was pulled out of bed every night how could he be expected to be at drill every morning, or any other complaint. He had himself complained that Perry was late for drill, but he had never given that reason for being late. Perry asked how, if the reprimand had been strongly expressed as he claimed, Maxwell himself had shortly afterwards given orders in Perry's presence for Lieutenant Dunscombe to be brought downstairs from his bedroom, between 1 and 2 o'clock in the morning, before the colonel and guests, in his shirt?

Maxwell repeated that the reprimand had been so strongly expressed that the only instance of a practical joke afterwards was that involving Dunscombe, but Maxwell had never ordered it but on the contrary went outside the anteroom to prevent the young gentlemen bringing him in. The door was burst open by the party carrying him and Maxwell was carried in to the room along with them. Colonel Garrett was sitting with his back to the door, and though he would have heard the laughter to the best of Maxwell's knowledge he did not see Dunscombe. Dunscombe appealed to Maxwell, saying 'Major, will you stand this?' and I told the youngsters to bundle out of the room. Dunscombe appeared in his uniform about five minutes afterwards.

The court adjourned for the day and resumed on Wednesday as the cross-examination of Major Maxwell continued. Maxwell knew nothing of any further instances of officers being pulled out of bed, but several companies had gone on detachment and he had stayed at Weedon with headquarters. When Perry mentioned a specific case of Hammond who had been brought into the mess-room, placed on the table and asked to sing a song, Maxwell had a slight recollection of this, now that it was brought to his memory, at Weedon. He had not then given a severe reprimand as he did not think it necessary. If it had been he would have given one. He agreed that he had occasionally had private letters from Perry but these were asking leave from parade and drills, and he never kept such notes.

Questioned by the court, Maxwell did not know if Hammond had been pulled out of bed and brought by force, but he had never made any complaint. He did not recollect how he was dressed. Perry had gone on detachment about five months after the third complaint. He never heard of another complaint from him. Maxwell believed that Garrett could not have called Perry a fool as he never spoke to an officer on any point of duty except in the presence of one of the majors, or senior officers, and the adjutant.

Perry asked if the colonel had used unmeasured language to Dunscombe. Maxwell was sure he had not. Perry's third complaint had been in June or July 1853 and Hammond's case in April or May 1854. Perry had been on detachment from December 1853 until June 1854. Maxwell stood down. Perry asked if he might add to his list of witnesses and the President said he might call anyone he wished in his defence, in due course.

Major Fyffe knows nothing

Major Fyffe, 46th Regiment, was then called, and the prosecutor said he would be examined on the first two charges to save time. He had never heard the colonel call Perry a fool, and he knew nothing of any letter to the colonel threatening him. He was not present when the colonel had adjudicated on Perry's complaint. The colonel might have received a letter without his knowledge. He was asked if another officer had actually sent a letter of complaint to the general of the district, and had been roundly abused the next morning by the colonel before all the officers, captains and subalterns. Before Fyffe could answer the court was cleared and the question was considered. On readmission it was put. Fyffe said he could not answer that from his own knowledge. He did not remember anyone telling him about it, nor was he present when Colonel Garrett read Dunscombe's letter. (It was presumably, therefore, Dunscombe who had written to the general.)

Perry asked whether Fyffe had spoken to anyone in the short recess about the question which had been read to the court before the adjournment. Fyffe said he had mentioned it to two or three officers. Pressed he said these were Mr Curtis and Captain Campbell but he merely said the question was about Dunscombe's business. This was a reference to the report in *The Times* of Colonel Garrett's answer yesterday, which had been the subject of conversation between the officers that morning. He paused and then said it was not that answer he meant. He intended to refer to another. He was under a wrong impression of Colonel Garrett's answer. He meant another occurrence in which he had previously heard of a letter written by Dunscombe. Perry pointed out to the court that the witness had changed his answer three times. Pressed he agreed that he had heard in the course of casual conversation that Lieutenant Dunscombe had complained to the General of the district by letter. He thought that it was as a result of being brought from his bed, but he did not know if he was brought to the anteroom, but could not recollect the time, nor where it took place.

Fyffe told the court he was not aware of Perry being persecuted after the reprimand to the subaltern officers, nor that Perry was ever called names. If his company was studiously avoided it was not because he had complained, but from his general temper. Fyffe hesitated, It was a difficult question to answer. He himself did not care for him as he did not admire his general disposition and temper.

Sandwith speaks

After a ten minute adjournment Captain Sandwith, 46th, was called. He had been adjutant in Dublin except for an absence of ten or twelve days. He had never heard Garrett call Perry a fool, or reprimand him for complaining, and knew nothing of a letter to the general. He had no reason to believe that Perry had ever been persecuted.

Perry put it to him that all this could have taken place without Sandwith's knowledge due to his absence and that as a married officer he lived outside barracks. Sandwith disagreed. The things mentioned could not have taken place without him knowing. Perry objected that the witness was arguing but the court ruled that his answer, good or bad, must be accepted.

Did Sandwith know that Perry had been pulled out of bed several times, Waldy's and Knapp's rooms had been turned upside down, Dunscombe ill-treated more than once, and Hammond placed on the mess table at Weedon? Sandwith said he did not know about Perry, or Waldy and Knapp. He knew that Dunscombe was once pulled out of his bed. He had complained to the colonel who severely reprimanded the officers concerned in the presence of all the officers. He thought that Hammond had never been ill-treated since joining the regiment. He did not think the colonel had said anything to Dunscombe when reprimanding his tormentors. It was too long ago for him to remember.

Perry asked what Sandwith knew about Dunscombe's letter. Was it to the colonel, or through the colonel to the general. Sandwith said it was to the colonel only but he doubted if it was still in the orderly room files as the regiment had moved three times since it was written and it was the practice then to destroy all useless letters.

The court asked how Colonel Garrett had spoken to Perry when he had complained of ill-treatment. The witness did not recollect the colonel speaking to Perry at that time. Was Perry's society shunned by the other officers? Sandwith thought that his society was not sought, due to his disagreeable manner. His swaggering manner, leading one to suppose he was a man of enormous - the witness did not finish. He was contemptuous of anything military or regimental. His supposed debauched habits, and latterly from ill-conduct in a monetary transaction. Perry said he wanted to ask Sandwith another question as he had attacked his character without the slightest chance of proving the truth of his assertions. The President said that the better way would be to call witnesses to disprove Sandwith's testimony.

Sandwith had not been present when Garrett had reprimanded officers over Perry's complaint and had no recollection of it. Perry now put in another question and the President said it might be put, but he thought that it would be better to make the point in another way. Perry agreed, and said that fortunately he had the whole of the letters connected with the money matters and he would be sorry if such personal matters were brought before the court as it related to purchasing steps in the regiment. He would take other means of publicly refuting the aspersions cast upon his character by this witness.

Nicholas answers

Captain Nicholas was then called, and confirmed that he had never heard Garrett call Perry a fool for his pains, or reproach him for making complaints. He had never heard that Perry had sent a letter to the colonel threatening to complain to the general. He thought that the persecution of Perry had stopped when the colonel reprimanded the officer who had been responsible. The court adjourned.

On resumption at eleven o'clock on Thursday, 3rd August, the prosecutor announced that he had no more questions for Nicholas and the previous evidence was read over to the witness. Perry asked if he could hand in a written statement, and Dalgetty, the Deputy Judge Advocate read it. Perry noted with regret that the public papers had remarked adversely on the way the court-martial had been conducted. He wished to say that he had received from it the greatest kindness and indulgence. He proceeded to cross-examine Captain Nicholas. Nicholas admitted that he had gone to Perry's room on the night that the 21st Fusiliers had dined at the Barracks but he had not heard, nor had he made, any request to Perry not to complain to the general of the district. There had been no other officer present. When he had arrived an officer from another regiment had been in the room but he had left as soon as Nicholas entered. Perry put it to him that he had put on his coatee to try to report personally to the commanding officer. Nicholas had not seen this, nor ever heard of it until he had read it in *The Times* newspaper. Nor had he seen Lieutenant Waldy in the room. The officer from another regiment already referred to was Lieutenant Trevelyan of the 11th Hussars but there had been no mention of reporting to the general. Perry insisted that Waldy had been there but Nicholas was firm that he had never seen him.

Perry turned to another matter. Had Lieutenant Dunscombe been brought down to the mess-room in his shirt by the express order of Major Maxwell? Was the colonel in the room? Nicholas said 'not on that night', but Perry said he did not specify any particular night. Nicholas then remembered Dunscombe being brought into the room by some officers in his shirt. He had not heard Major Maxwell go and order them to bring him down, but when there was a noise outside the anteroom door Maxwell had gone to see what it was and he had been swept back in with a rush as the other officers brought Dunscombe in. He had heard Major Maxwell say 'Take him out of this', or 'This is no place for him', or somesuch words. The young officers had immediately taken Dunscombe away. The whole affair had taken but a few seconds and though Colonel Garrett was in the room he had his back towards the door. Nicholas denied that he had helped to execute the orders and had been the one who named the officers sent for Dunscombe. Had Perry not been sitting in the room, near Major Maxwell, at the time? Nicholas could not recollect where Perry had been, but he had not ordered any officers to go and get Dunscombe. He agreed that the officers concerned had been in the anteroom before they had left to bring him down. Perry had no more questions.

The court asked why Nicholas had gone to Perry's room, and if to deliver orders what were they? Nicholas said that Colonel Garrett had received a note, and had passed it to Major Maxwell to read. One of them, he was not sure which, had then asked him to go to Perry's room to see what was the matter. The officer of the 11th Hussars had been there. Nicholas had asked 'what is the matter here?' and the 11th Hussar had left. Perry had said that he had been pulled out of his bed. Nicholas had said that he did not appear to have suffered much and his bed seemed all right again. Perry who was in his shirt had said that he had put the bed together again himself. Nicholas told him to go to bed and that he would caution the officers not to go near his room again. In the passage he had met several officers - he could not recollect who - and had desired them not to go near Perry's room again that night. He had returned to the anteroom and had told Major Maxwell what he had seen and what he had done. He thought Maxwell had passed this on to the colonel.

The court asked why he had spoken thus to the other officers? Had he feared more disturbance? Nicholas said that it was late and he thought officers might go to Perry to ask what had happened. There had been a public dinner in the mess that night. He had not heard of any officers returning to Perry's room, nor of any further annoyance to him. He thought Perry had been satisfied with the way in which his complaint that night had been settled.

To further questions from the court Nicholas said that he had been present some time later when an officer had been severely reprimanded by the colonel and ordered him never to enter Perry's room, by day or night. He had never heard that Perry had been subjected to annoyance after this reprimand. He was asked if Perry had been shunned by his brother officers. He did not think him on terms of intimacy with his brother officers and there was not the same feeling towards him as to others. He had a disagreeable kind of manner - a peculiar forwardness about him. Nicholas said that Perry's note merely stated that he had been pulled out of bed. It contained no threat.

M'Alester recalled

Lieutenant and Adjutant M'Alester was then recalled and the second charge was read. M'Alester had not been present when the colonel reprimanded an officer for annoying Perry, and had never heard the colonel reproach Perry for making complaints or call him a fool for his pains. Nor had he any knowledge of Perry, either by word of mouth or in writing, threatening to complain against the colonel to the general of the district. Perry asked if M'Alester recollected Dunscombe threatening to appeal to the general of the district? M'Alester said nothing except by hearsay as he had been on duty at the Pigeon-house at the time. He agreed that Dunscombe's letter had been the subject of discussion in the regiment, for it had been improperly worded and the colonel had reprimanded him. The Deputy Judge Advocate asked if he knew this of his own knowledge. M'Alester did not. He had heard the letter talked of and that the colonel had reprimanded Dunscombe, not for making the complaint, but for improperly wording it. Perry asked if it had not also been the subject of conversation in the regiment that he too had written a letter to the colonel threatening to complain to the general of the district. M'Alester had never heard it. Perry asked if he had been called the 'malefactor' after complaining to the colonel. M'Alester thought that he may have been called that, but it was not his nickname. Perry did not press for an answer.

The court asked if Perry's company had been shunned by his brother officers, and if so was it for having complained to the colonel? M'Alester thought he had been disliked in the regiment but he himself had never shunned his society; those who had could give their own reasons. To his knowledge Perry had not been subjected to annoyance or persecution after the officer who had done so had been reprimanded by the colonel. Perry asked if there had not been a time immediately after his complaint when he had been virtually 'sent to Coventry'? M'Alester said no.

Dunscombe toes the party line

The next witness was Lieutenant Dunscombe. He had been in the regiment since 23rd November 1852 and had been present with the other officers in Dublin when the colonel had reprimanded an officer after a complaint from Perry. The colonel had not reproached Perry, nor had he called him a fool for his pains. He had no knowledge of Perry threatening to complain to the general of the district. Dunscombe said that he had on occasion been annoyed by other officers forcing their way into his room and pulling him out of bed. Perry himself had done this, in Manchester, earlier this year, at the end of April or early May. Perry and another officer had come to his room and smashed in the door. Perry had been rather drunk He had not been pulled out of bed on that occasion. Perry asked how he could say that he had done it? He had told him the next day that he had not, and the other officer had admitted to Dunscombe that he had done it. Dunscombe did not remember the other officer saying so, and he believed that Perry had done it.

Perry then asked Dunscombe if, since the enquiry had been instituted and it was known that Dunscombe would be required to give evidence, he had spoken to anyone on the subject of the evidence he should give, and if so to whom? Dunscombe declined to answer the question and a derisive murmur passed through the court. Perry said in that case he had no more questions.

The court asked if Perry had ever pulled Dunscombe out of bed. He had not. The only time he had been annoyed by Perry was on that occasion. Perry had entered his room. Lieutenant Waldy was the other officer involved. He had been pulled out of bed on one other occasion, but not by Perry. He had been dragged out and brought to the ante-room against his will. It had happened some time last October when the regiment was at the Royal Barracks, Dublin. He did not think that Colonel Garrett had seen him. Major Maxwell had not been part of the party, nor had Perry. Later, he had written a letter to the colonel, or perhaps the adjutant, threatening to complain to the general and had been reprimanded for it. He was young in the service at the time and had been blamed for making the threat before applying to the colonel. Perry had not joined in practical jokes by other officers, but he did not think he was shunned by other officers. That concluded the evidence of Dunscombe and the court adjourned.

The court reassembled on its seventh day, Friday 4th August, and *The Times* reporter was to record the next day that Perry, the prisoner, looked pale and careworn. He was still attended by his legal adviser, Mr Darvill, Town Clerk of Windsor. Before the court was opened a lengthy discussion took place among the members and the court was cleared for half-an-hour. When the public were re-admitted the court was formally opened, and Perry asked for Dunscombe's answer to his last question to be read. This was, of course, the one about discussing his evidence which Dunscombe had declined to answer. Perry said that he would ask that in future the questions to witnesses not be read aloud until the witness was to answer. So far the Deputy Judge Advocate had read out the question, entered it in writing in the record, and then put it to the witness. The President pointed out that that procedure had been adopted at Perry's request so that he could write the questions down. Perry agreed, but said that circumstances had changed since then, but he would not press the point.

Curtis reveals the colonel's questionnaire, and the meeting of officers

Lieutenant Curtis was called and sworn. The first two charges against Perry were read over to him. In July 1853 he had been with the regiment in the Linen-hall Barracks, Dublin, and had heard the officer reprimanded for annoying Perry. He was positive that Colonel Garrett had not reproached Perry nor called him a fool for his pains. He did not recollect any confidential circulars about practical jokes being read to the officers at that time. He did not know if Perry had ever sent a letter to the colonel threatening to complain to the general. Perry cross-examined. Had Curtis, since this enquiry had been started, been spoken to about the evidence he would give? If so, by whom? And had he any conversations about the evidence? Curtis had not been spoken to but had gathered the general tenor of the evidence from the newspapers. Perry asked about a circular that Colonel Garrett had sent round to the officers just before this enquiry had begun. Curtis could not produce a copy, but said that the colonel had sent round three questions to some officers, and two to others, to be answered and returned to the orderly room. He thought that these had been taken to Horse Guards. The prosecutor pointed out that he had not explained what was in the circular. Curtis said that each officer had been asked if he could remember the colonel reproach Perry for complaining, or call him a fool for his pains. Had any officer heard that Perry had threatened to write to the general to complain? Finally did any know of the ill-usage alleged by Perry to have been done to young officers by Captain Nicholas? These were the three questions put to Curtis.

Perry asked if there had been any discussion as to the evidence he should give. Had he been spoken to about Dunscombe's evidence yesterday, and what was said by other officers about that evidence? Curtis said that there was conversation each morning on the evidence as it appeared in the papers. There had been no discussion about the evidence he should give and he had heard no opinion on Dunscombe's evidence. Perry pressed him. Was he aware that some officers were constantly asking others what answers they should give to the circular from the colonel. Curtis admitted that there was a conversation among officers about the circular, before the court-martial was ordered. Perry appealed to the court: was that a complete answer to his question? Curtis said he could answer more fully. He had received the questions at about 9 o'clock in the morning. He went round to Lieutenant Waldy's room and found him answering the questions. He said 'these are very simple questions to be answered' and returned to his own room where he wrote his answers and gave them to the adjutant. Perry asked if the 'officers' assembly' had been sounded, and if the officers had all been called together to refresh each others' memory. Curtis said 'certainly not'. Perry asked why he had gone to Waldy if the questions were so simple? Curtis said to see if he had the same questions to answer. Perry pressed him on the officers' assembly. Had the officers not been in deliberation about an hour? Now Curtis said that on reconsideration he thought the officers' assembly had sounded, but he forgot which day. It was for the auditing of the mess accounts.

Perry suggested that the accounts were at hand and asked that they be produced. The President said that Colonel Garrett would be recalled later and could be asked for them. Perry asked Curtis again about the time of the officers' assembly. Curtis said that it was a day or two before the court-martial assembled. On the day that Colonel Garrett went to Horse Guards, in fact. Perry said that he thought it singular that the mess accounts should have been audited at that particular time. The President agreed.

Perry asked Curtis if he had not spoken to him after the reprimand, in Curtis's room, and hadn't Curtis said: 'I think you've got the worst of reporting, old fellow', and hadn't Perry promised not to report any more. Curtis could not recollect the circumstances, but thought it might have happened. He did not deny it. Perry asked him again when the mess accounts had been last audited. Had it not been done on July 9th, shortly before? Curtis said he must respectfully decline to answer the question, as he could not swear to the day, and because it did not bear on the case.

The court asked him if Perry had been subjected to any annoyance or persecution after officers had been reprimanded by the colonel for annoying him. Curtis had no knowledge of any. Shortly afterwards Perry had gone on the sick list and had been in hospital for over three months. Perry had not been in the habit of joining in practical jokes to his brother officers. Curtis did not think he was on sufficiently intimate terms to join in practical jokes. His society was not actually shunned but it was not courted. It was not on account of his having complained. He had not suffered at all to Curtis's knowledge for having made the complaint. The officers' assembly was not sounded every day, except for mess. Perry pointed out that the mess call was an entirely different call.

Through the court, as all his questions were, Perry asked if Dunscombe had been abused for having reported other officers, and had not Colonel Garrett used 'unmeasured abuse' towards him? Curtis had not been present as he had been on detachment with the Main Guard at Dublin. He had heard of it afterwards.

Hesketh reveals the true purpose of the officers' meeting

Lieutenant Hesketh was then called, and sworn. He was asked about the same matters as Curtis had been, and gave broadly similar answers until asked about the assembly of officers. He did not think that mess accounts had been audited. The assembly of officers was for Colonel Garrett to address them, and to remark on the falsehoods contained in the letter from Perry to Colonel the Hon A. Upton, President of Greer's Court-martial. This had been printed in *The Times*. The court adjourned for ten minutes. On its return it recalled Colonel Garrett.

Garrett recalled

Garrett said he had never received a letter from the prisoner threatening to complain to the general of the district. Perry had complained to him about three different annoyances taking place at the Linen-hall Barracks in Dublin in May and June, and perhaps into July 1853. Garrett had received a confidential circular from Horse Guards in July 1853 and had no doubt he would have read it to the officers. The officers ordered to go to Turkey had not been specially selected. He had intended that the two senior captains should each go with all his officers and his company. There had been little time for them to get ready as the order came on the Saturday for them to leave on the following Monday. Captain Wombwell's and Captain O'Toole's companies were at first warned. But the larger portion of Wombwell's company was on detachment at Kensington and Hyde Park. He therefore substituted Captain Hardy's company. The selection was not at all influenced by Perry's trial as he thought it was already sitting.

The prosecutor then asked Garrett to comment on the prisoner's arrrest and confinement. At the beginning of the trial Perry had complained that he was confined to a small room and this was injurious to his health as well as depressing to his spirits. Perry intervened to say that the colonel had given permission for him to walk in his uniform in the barrack square and to go out with Mr Darvill whenever he wished. He had to thank the colonel for that permission. He had written to the Commander-in-Chief for permission to go outside the baracks, on his parole of honour.

A word of explanation may be helpful. As made clear in *Simmons on Courts-martial*[46], the authority referred to by Lieutenant Perry early in his trial, a court-martial has no control over the nature of the arrest of a prisoner, except as regards his personal freedom in court. An officer is put in arrest by the officer who orders it, usually by the adjutant when ordered by the commanding officer. On being placed in arrest he resigns his sword to the person imposing it, (and if this form be sometimes omitted it is considered nevertheless to have taken place), and it follows that an officer in arrest cannot wear a sword. Arrest of an officer was either close, which meant that the officer was confined to his quarters, or 'at large', that is extended to the garrison, camp or other defined limits - now invariably referred to as 'open arrest'. He could not, however, dine at his own or any other military mess, nor appear in any place of public amusement. Unless confined for some very heinous offence, an officer was not usually placed in the charge of a sentry, but was considered on parole. A court could not interfere, even with a view to facilitate his defence, to cause a close arrest to be relaxed to open arrest. The officer in command was alone responsible for the discharge of this duty. Thus in the present case, the arrest was ordered by Colonel Garrett who remained responsible for all consequences.

Colonel Garrett said that on the last day of the first trial, Major Pack had asked him whether Perry could take exercise at large. Garrett had answered that he desired to give him every possible liberty but he thought he would be deviating from the custom of the service if he allowed him to take exercise beyond the limits of the barrack square. The following day he was approached by Perry's legal adviser, who he now knew was Mr Darvill. Darvill asked that Perry be allowed to go outside barracks but he pointed out that this was impossible unless he went out

---

[46]See p118 et seq of the Fourth Edition, pub 1852.

under surveillance. Darvill asked Garrett if he knew who he was, and after some further conversation Garrett consented to Perry going in Darvill's carriage to Darvill's house which is in the country and quite private. Darvill promised to send him back during the course of the night. In the course of that evening Garrett received an extremely well expressed letter from Darvill and consented a second time to Perry going, this time with a gentleman from Darvill's house. Perry interjected that it was Darvill's son. Since that time, Perry has been out several times without application from Darvill and left his name in the orderly room with the hour of his going out and coming in. Today, permission has arrived from Lord Hardinge, the Commander-in-Chief, for him to go out on parole subject to certain restrictions.

Perry said that the colonel had behaved in the most courteous, kind and gentlemanly way in reference to his arrest and had done all in his power to mitigate such a state of discipline. The remarks of both Garrett and Perry were entered in the court record, and the latter began to cross-examine the former.

Garrett could not recollect Perry writing to him threatening to appeal to the general of the district, nor calling him a fool for his pains, and both were so marked that he could not fail to recollect them if they had occurred. He had not been 'anxious' about Perry's first trial as suggested by the prisoner. He agreed that he had written to one of the officers who had been at Cork with Perry to ask about his conduct while there but he did not remember whether he had specifically asked about gambling. Perry asked about Captain Hardy, and Lieutenant Shervinton, being sent to the East. Wasn't Hardy nearly at the bottom of the list of captains, and didn't Shervinton belong to K Company, not to Hardy's? Garrett said that when he found that he could not send Wombwell's company he made up his list from the juniors but could not send Captain Lyons and his company as he was also out at Kensington. Captain Hardy was above Lyons in the list. Garrett doubted if Lieutenant Hesketh had been present when the officers had been reprimanded.

The court asked if Garrett had assembled the officers after the letter from Perry had been quoted in *The Times*. He had. He had read out the letter, sentence by sentence, and had asked if any of them could assist him by mentioning any circumstance that could possibly be construed into a reproach to Perry, and also whether any of them knew of a letter sent to him containing threats. The court adjourned for the weekend.

Chapter 6 – Press Outrage

The Commander-in-Chief and his fellows at Horse Guards no doubt turned to their newspapers on Monday 7th August with apprehensive hearts, but hoping that for one day there would be no court-martial to read about. They were disappointed. There was, of course, the report of Saturday's proceedings and there was worse. For there was a biting leader, and a scathing letter from 'A Civilian'. The letter, which filled a complete column, purported to inform the public about the secret tribunals, 'courts of enquiry', which packed by the Horse Guards ensured that aristocratic and influential individual officers had always met with the most culpable indulgence, while the weak and friendless had always gone to the wall. He wrote that it had long been the habit of the half-educated members of our aristocracy and plutocracy, who on leaving public schools had felt themselves unequal to meet the educational tests requisite to qualify them for entering university, to take refuge in certain fashionable regiments in which they could dress gorgeously and play at soldiering with very slight chance of ever being called upon to perform any real service, and where they could agreeably divide their time between horseracing, betting, fornicating and prizefighting. They resented the appointment of any young man not thought to be 'in society' and resisted such intrusion by all means in their power, fair or foul. If the young man concerned, of course a mere lad of 16 or 17 years of age, should show any sign of mental or bodily weakness they would at once fall upon him and brutally drive him out. If he was strong and resolute they would send him to Coventry and nobody would speak to him. All this happens daily, as the Commander-in-

Chief well knows. A youth in such a 'swell' regiment might be condemned because he goes to bed early, because he says his prayers, because he is shocked by the presence of prostitutes, because he will not drink and smoke and swear, because he is shy, studious, or silent. If he is poor and chooses not to spend his money on eating, drinking or gambling, he may still have in him the making of an excellent soldier. When such incidents reach the notice of the Horse Guards, if they were invariably made the subject of open courts-martial, they would speedily die a violent death and a young officer would be allowed in future to live in peace and quiet and in any manner he pleased, so long as he did his duty attentively and manfully, and behaved in other respects like a gentleman. But instead they are settled by courts of inquiry, in secret, and the rich and influential bully escapes with impunity and the system endures. For the courts of inquiry are invariably composed of officers who entirely approve the system and they decide that, although the assailants have gone too far and ought to be reprimanded, the victim will not 'do' for the army and must sell out. The bullies have therefore attained their object, and a reprimand is a mere harmless formality. The writer gave a specific instance of an officer in a fashionable regiment who resisted attempts to drive him out and 'called out' (for a duel) his principal tormentor. The bully refused to fight until insulted in the street, and a bloodless exchange of shots followed. A court of inquiry hushed up the matter, for the regiment contained many lords' sons, on condition that the persecution of the victim ceased. But the officer who had behaved so honourably was 'sent to Coventry' by the bully's cronies and no one would speak to him. He survived this objectionable treatment for several years before selling out. Even officers joining the regiment long after the original affair cravenly took the easy way and did not speak to him. The correspondent warmed to his subject! He suggested that several of the offending officers had since married prostitutes and retired into private life, others had been obliged to flee the country for swindling on the turf. Repeated courts of inquiry had hushed up orgies which ought to have broken up the regiment, and must have done so if they had been inquired into publicly. Not one of the officers had been heard of in the service as a gallant or good soldier. In another regiment at the very time of writing an officer who was the son of a solicitor was being shunned by his fellows, not by any means all sprung from the nobility, and had lived alone in his regiment for nearly two years. It appears that his father had lent money to the commanding officer of the regiment, and his lieutenancy was said to be a repayment for the loan. They had not the wit to see, that if the story be true, it was a reflection on the colonel, not on the young man. The examples which these worthless regiments had set had now penetrated into the line and in the 46th the officers were determined to stand by each other and to allow no 'slow coaches' to thrive in their society. As yet we had glimpsed little of that society, but he trusted that the courts-martial of Colonel Garrett and Major Maxwell, which must surely follow, would let us see more.

The letter clearly shows how a case may be weakened by what was clearly exaggeration and unconcealed prejudice. The newspaper's leader was equally biting but more restrained and consequently more effective. A writer of travels, now many years back, had written about certain Arabian tribes, including the people of Muscat. He had dismissed them in a few words: 'As for manners, they have none; and their customs are abominable.' If a writer in our own time wished to convey to his readers a good idea of the tone which pervades the society of officers in certain regiments of the British army, they noted with pain, then he could do no better than adopt the precise words of the historian of Muscat. Could anything be more purely disgraceful, disgusting and humiliating than the revelations which had taken place in the course of the various Windsor courts-martial? Leave aside the fate of the luckless youth who was so unfortunate as to receive a commission in the 46th Regiment, for that affected but one individual. But if the court-martial reached an unjust decision it would affix a deeper stigma on the character of the British officer than it has yet received. It would prove to the world that the various acts of brutality which had been reported were not exceptional cases, they were not the results of extraordinary ruffianism in the subalterns and extraordinary neglect on the part of the commanding officer. They would receive the sanction of the Horse Guards. The court had to decide whether the officers of the English army are henceforth to be considered gentlemen, or not. Any one who had perused the evidence would readily form a judgement on the brutal attack to which young Perry was subjected. It would be a sorry sight indeed if a court of English officers, the Commander-in-Chief and the Queen herself effectively approved the attack by denying the young officer the right to defend himself against the last indignity which can be offered to a mangy cur. There was something disheartening in the appointment of this second court-martial even before the decision of the first was known. The prisoner was put to a near impossible proof, and no rational man would pay any serious attention to the statements of half-a-dozen officers who stepped forward to swear, one after another, that they didn't remember. Every man knew that the man who should really be on trial was Colonel Garrett under whose auspices such disgraceful irregularities had occurred. He should be required to answer for the condition of his regiment. And now there were two military commissions of inquiry into the conduct of officers in other regiments which was said to be as bad as that in the 46th. The writer's own experience of life had not been that of the barrack and mess-room, but in no public school in the country, in neither university, and in no circle of young men in London who aspire to the character of gentlemen, had one ever heard of such scenes of ruffianism and vice as appear to have prevailed in certain corps in the Queen's service. It seemed that a deplorable tone of debauchery prevailed among the younger officers of the army. Of course there were many exceptions and in every regiment there were to be found young men of gentlemanly temper and cleaner minds, who looked upon such scenes as those described with disgust and abhorrence. The character of a regiment depends on that of the commanding officer, and in many the commanding officers did their duty and the regiments were entirely free from the taint of violent immorality or ruffianism. It was not enough to maintain decency at the mess-table and on parade. The weight of the commanding officer's character must be felt and subalterns must display that influence in their manners and conduct. Every now and then a black sheep will creep into the regiment and he must be got rid of as quickly as possible. If he is fit to command, by his own life he set before his officers the example of that conduct which it was right that they should pursue. It is that influence which Colonel Garrett appears to have neglected.

The Eighth Day

Finally, there was the report of Saturday's proceedings, the eighth day. The paper commented on the intense interest in the inquiry shown by the increased attendance of the public. Although the room used was the largest in the barracks, it was almost completely occupied by the members' table and the accomodation for the Deputy Judge-Advocate, prosecutor and prisoner so that there was standing room for only about a dozen persons. On Saturday however double that number choked up the doorway and passage and among them were Colonel the Hon Foster MP, Captain Bulkeley, Captain H. Seymour, and two private friends of the prisoner 'whose names did not transpire'. The court assembled at 11 o'clock, and was formally opened by the Deputy Judge-Advocate. The examination of Colonel Garrett was then resumed and he was asked if there had been an inspection by the general officer after the incident of the reprimand given by Garrett to the officers who had annoyed Perry and, if so, whether Perry had complained to the general of any ill-treatment. Garrett said that the last inspection had been in Dublin by the general there, Major General Cochrane, in, he thought, October 1853. He thought Perry had been present but he had made no complaint. The Court asked about Garrett's assembly of the officers after Perry's letter to Colonel Upton had appeared in the papers. Had Lieutenant Curtis been present? Garrett thought he had. Perry then asked, through the court, if he had not withdrawn his letter of complaint to the general at Garrett's request, and because he did not wish to ruin any young man's prospects. He had done so on condition that the man concerned was reprimanded severely. Garrett could not remember ever having received such a letter from Perry. That concluded the case for the prosecution on Charges 1 and 2, and the Deputy Judge-Advocate then read Charges 3 and 4. The third charge was of scandalous, infamous conduct unbecoming an officer and a gentleman, by stating in his evidence in Greer's trial that Captain Nicholas had not reprimanded officers who had bullied him and he, Captain Nicholas himself, had ill-treated officers on first joining, when the last phrase was false.

The fourth charge was similar and related to a letter sent during Greer's trial by Perry to the Deputy Judge-Advocate, in which Perry had said that Nicholas himself ill-treated young officers and aided and abetted others doing so, when he knew that was false.

The prosecutor placed a certified copy of the proceedings in Greer's trial before the court and Lieutenant Colonel Pipon, who had been Deputy Judge-Advocate in that trial was called and sworn. Perry attempted to intervene to say that in writing to Colonel Pipon he had only been doing what Major Pack, the Deputy Judge-Advocate in his own (the first) trial had told him he had a right to do. The President said that the letter was not yet before the court, but Pipon confirmed that he had acted in the

Greer trial and had received a letter from Perry and it was then produced. It read:

'Sir, I am humbly submit that I am the virtual prosecutor in this case, as Colonel Garrett, the nominal prosecutor, declines to put questions necessary to the elucidation of the truth, I ask to have the opportunity of cross-examining witnesses. I understand that Major Maxwell has stated on oath that Captain Nicholas never ill-treated young officers. Were I allowed the opportunity, I could put questions to prove that he did, and that he aids and abets nearly everything of the kind that takes place, Yours etc,

JE Perry, Lieutenant 46th Regiment, Windsor Barracks, July 21.'

Perry stated that he had written the letter of his own free will, and had signed it and sent it to the Deputy Judge-Advocate in that trial without consulting anybody.

The Deputy Judge-Advocate read the extract from that trial in which Perry had said the words listed in the fourth charge. Perry said that the questions and answers before and after that particular one materially qualified them. They would show that the answer he gave was extracted from him contrary to his wish. He had objected at first but was told that he must answer. The words were put into his mouth, but he did not deny that he did answer so, and was prepared to prove that answer true.

'Nicholas was always kind'

A series of young officers of the 46th were then called in turn and asked basically the same questions. First was Ensign Henry Lawson who had been in the regiment only about four months. Next came Ensign Henry Carr William Hammond who had joined in March 1853, Ensign Richard Coote who had been in the 46th since 10 January 1854 and Ensign George Morland Hutton who had been in the regiment about ten months. Finally

109

THE WINDSOR COURTS-MARTIAL

Lieutenant W. T. Waldy was sworn. All denied ever being ill-treated by Captain Nicholas, and were sure that he had never aided and abetted others in annoying young officers. He had apparently always been ready to give young officers advice and assisted them in every possible way. He had always treated them with the greatest possible kindness. None had experienced any practical jokes. Hammond denied Perry's suggestion that he had been pulled out of bed, placed on the mess table, and made to sing a song. Nor did he know of any other officer being treated so. He also denied that he had been told what to say in evidence. Before entering the room he had no idea what he would be asked.

Waldy and his letter

Coote denied that Nicholas had called him 'son of a --- of an ensign'. Waldy was asked if he had heard Nicholas call another officer this, or any other opprobious epithets. He did not remember anything of the sort. Perry pressed him on this but Waldy remained firm. Had he ever said that Nicholas had used such words? Waldy replied that as he had never heard Captain Nicholas use such words, he most decidedly never could have said so. Perry asked him if he had not stated in writing that he had used the words. Waldy said, never to his knowledge. Perry then handed up a letter to the President and asked if the signature could be shown to the witness, but no other part of the letter, and that it not be read. The President replied that they could make no compromise with him, and if a letter is put in then the whole of it must be read. Perry said he wished to put it in as part of his defence and was only cross-examining for the moment. The letter was handed to the President who read its contents with great surprise, his countenance evidently denoting that the words said to have been used by Captain Nicholas formed part of its contents. Waldy was shown the letter and agrees that the whole of it was in his writing. Perry asked for the letter back, but the Deputy Judge-

Advocate said that he would keep it safe, but it must not leave the court. Perry, advised by Mr Darvill asked to argue the point, and the court was cleared for an hour and a quarter. The Deputy Judge-Advocate then said that the court would retain the letter but it would not be read unless demanded by the prisoner. The latter could make a copy of it if he wished so that he could make use of it, but Perry did not wish to. The court and Perry sealed the original letter. He then asked Waldy again if Captain Nicholas had used the words alleged. Waldy replied that he stated the same as before: he had not the slightest remembrance of it.

Perry had no more questions but the court asked if Waldy remembered any officer being reprimanded by Colonel Garrett for annoying Perry. Waldy had not been present at any such event. He could not say if Perry had been subject to annoyance or persecution after the reprimand as he did not know when a reprimand had been given. Since he had been in the regiment he did not know of any annoyance towards Perry. The court asked if Perry had ever joined in practical jokes towards his brother officers? Waldy said that he and Perry had once been together to Lieutenant Dunscombe's room, where they had wakened him up. The court asked if the door had been smashed in, but Waldy did not think it had, but could not be certain. Perry had never joined in a practical joke against Waldy, but was once in the room when Waldy was woken up in the same way as Dunscombe was. (Laughter.) There was no ill-will on anybody's part.

Dunscombe was then called and sworn but before he could say anything the court adjourned as it was four o'clock. While the newspaper's readers, including all the members of the court and the officers of the regiment, digested all the unpalatable remarks in the letters and leading article, the court reconvened on Monday, 7 August, its ninth day.

More officers with poor memories

Dunscombe, who had been sworn on Friday, began his evidence. He too had never experienced any ill-treatment from Captain Nicholas, whom he considered always very kind to young officers on joining. He had never heard the captain use opprobious names to officers who had reported problems. Perry pressed him. Had Nicholas not, the day after Dunscombe had sent an official report to the general commanding the district, and in Perry's presence, called Dunscombe 'a d--- son of a b---' and 'a b----' for reporting? The witness had never heard Captain Nicholas make use of such expressions, nor did he remember going to Perry's room and saying that the officers could call him what names they liked, but he didn't care. Perry asked him if it was not true that many of the officers had cut him for reporting to the general of the district. Dunscombe agreed that a few of the officers had been cool to him for a few days, but he did not report to the general.

Perry changed tack. He asked who was present when Dunscombe had been pulled out of bed by his cousin, Captain Webb? Dunscombe could not remember, and pressed he could not recall if Captain Nicholas was amongst them. Perry asked when the Webb incident had occurred, and when Dunscombe had gone to Perry's room after parade. Dunscombe thought that he had been pulled out of bed in June 1853, but as he could not remember having gone to Perry's room, he obviously could not remember the date. As near as he could recollect, he had sent in an official letter threatening to complain to the district in October 1853. He had never heard Ensign Stretton, who had left the regiment, saying that he would be revenged for indignities heaped upon him by Captain Nicholas. He could not remember when Stretton had left the regiment.

Line Infantry 1854

| Reporters. | Lieut. Perry. | Sergeant. | Mr. Darvill. Legal Adviser. |

The Court-Martial on Lieut. Perry of H. Majesty's 46th

EXAMIN.

LIEUT. WALDY DENIES HAVING EVER HEARD CAPTAIN NICHOLAS MAKE USE OF OPPROBRIOUS LANGUAGE TO AN
WHEREIN HE (LIEUT. WALDY) DISTINCTLY STATES THAT CAPTAIN NICHOLAS APPLIED THE DISGUSTING I
WRITTEN LETTER AND HIS STATEMENT ON OATH; AND ALSO *TOTALLY UNABLE TO RECOL*
CAPT. NICHOLAS OR TO THEMSELVES, OR IN

London: Lithographed from an Original Sketch, and Published Sept. 9th, 1854, by Read &

| Sergeant. | | Major Dalgetty, | Lieut. Waldy. | Col. Kelly, | General Wetherall, |
| Members of the Court. | | Deputy Judge Advocate. | | President. | Prosecutor. |

Regiment, in the Mess Room at Windsor Barracks, August 1854.

TION OF LIEUT. W. T. WALDY.

YOUNG OFFICER, OR THAT HE HAD EVER SO STATED IN WRITING. LIEUT. PERRY HANDING HIS LETTER TO THE PRESIDENT
*GUAGE REFERRED TO. TO ENSIGN COOTE. LIEUT. WALDY IS UNABLE TO PERCEIVE THE DISCREPANCY BETWEEN HIS
T, AS IS THE CASE WITH ALL HIS OTHER GALLANT BROTHER OFFICERS, ANYTHING PREJUDICIAL TO
E SLIGHTEST DEGREE ADVANTAGEOUS TO THE PRISONER

10, Johnson's Court, Fleet Street; and may be had of all Printsellers and Stationers in the United Kingdom.

SELLING OUT.

A Question. "MY GOOD FELLOW, I THINK I SHALL SELL OUT. WILL YOU BUY MY COMMISSION? HAVE IT A BARGAIN."

An Answer. "WHY, THANK'EE, OBLIGED FOR THE OFFER; BUT THE FACT IS, ALL MY LIFE I'VE BEEN 'CUSTOMED TO THE SOCIETY OF GEN'L'MEN."

The court asked who Captain Webb was. Was he an officer of the 46th at the time? Dunscombe explained that he had never served in the regiment. He was a captain in the 4th Dragoon Guards. The court also asked if his letter of complaint to Colonel Garrett had named any officers. Dunscombe had complained of four, including Greer and Knapp, but could not remember the other two. Captain Nicholas was not one of them, nor was Perry. He had never heard Perry reproached for complaining to Colonel Garrett, nor did he think he had suffered in any way. The court asked why Perry was so unpopular with his brother officers. Dunscombe could not say. Perry asked if Greer was not under arrest, and Knapp in Turkey. They were, and Dunscombe was asked why his memory was so clear about those two officers, and so oblivious as to others who had been present. Dunscombe said that it was because of those circumstances that their names were impressed on his memory. The witness was stood down.

Lieutenant George Frederick Dallas was sworn. He had been in the regiment a little over nine years. Like his younger colleagues he thought Captain Nicholas above reproach, and nothing could exceed his kindness and courtesy to his brother officers, young officers and all. He had seen very little of Lieutenant Perry, having been generally in other quarters but thought he was unpopular in the regiment due to his offensive forward manners and from his bad character. He did not really know and had only heard so. The President said this would not do. Perry intervened to say that there was no doubt of his own unpopularity in the regiment. The court asked Dallas if he had ever been the subject of practical jokes, and the prisoner asked if he had engaged in practical jokes against him. Dallas thought, to the best of his recollection, not. Nor could he remember a joke which Perry put to him, when Dallas had asked Perry to go out one evening, and had told him to dress to do so, but when Perry

113

had done so he had found his hat all broken. Dallas thought that he had possibly done this: he did not recollect.

The War intervenes

There was suddenly a dramatic moment, when the prosecutor, General Wetherall, announced that he had just received a letter from Colonel Garrett. Thirty men and a subaltern were to go out to the Crimea on *Harbinger* immediately and Dallas was the subaltern appointed. Wetherall asked Perry if he would need Dallas for his defence, but Perry said he had one or two questions, and then Dallas could go. Dallas denied that he was one of the subalterns who had broken open Perry's door in the Linenhall Barracks in Dublin, and had made him get into his tub. He agreed somewhat lukewarmly that Perry might have volunteered to do his duty when nobody else would when he wished to go away.

Lieutenant Forde, who had been in the regiment one year and eight months was then sworn. He repeated the familiar testimony to Captain Nicholas's high character and kindness to junior officers. On joining he had received from him more kindness and good nature than from anyone else. Forde had never been the subject of any practical jokes. When Perry asked him about being pulled out of bed in Dublin by Ensign Castles of the 17th Regiment, in the company of officers from the 46th, Forde denied this. Castles had come to his room, had talked to him for some time and had then attempted to pull off the bedclothes. This had annoyed Forde so he had got out of bed and turned him out. Greer of the 46th had been present. He denied that Curtis and Payne were also present. Greer had also tried to get hold of the bedclothes and he had also been turned out. Perry asked if this had happened the first night he himself had joined? Forde did not recollect.

Curtis's fond, but selective, memories

Lieutenant Curtis was then recalled. He, too, had the fondest memories of Captain Nicholas who had been kind to all young officers, but especially to Curtis himself. Perry asked how he could talk with such accuracy about such matters when on Friday last he had stated that the meeting of officers had been held to audit the mess accounts, when it had since transpired that it had been held for a very different purpose. Curtis said that he had totally forgotten on Friday that such a meeting had been held. Curtis also said, in response to what was put to him by Perry, that he did not remember that on Perry's first night in the regiment he had been taken up to Forde's room, where the door was broken open and Forde was taken from his bed. He agreed that Ensign Castles of the 17th Regiment had gone to Forde's room but on seeing an officer of another regiment, Forde had got out of bed and thrust him out. He had said that he did not mind it from officers of his own regiment, but would not stand it from others. Perry said that there were two other officers of the 46th there besides himself. The court asked if Captain Nicholas was one? He was not. The court now referred to Curtis's earlier testimony when he had, when Perry had come to his room, addressed him as 'old fellow'. They wondered if this was an expression which one officer could address to another whose society he intended to shun. Curtis said that he and Perry had not been on speaking terms for some months and when it was time for the regiment to leave Dublin, for Kilkenny outquarters, Perry had asked another officer to intervene and to propose to Curtis that they make it up, and Perry had come to his room and they had shaken hands on it. He might have used the term 'old fellow' at that time. The court adjourned for ten minutes.

More fond memories

On re-assembly Lieutenant Llewellyn was sworn. He had been in the regiment since 14 December 1849. He too had the fondest memories of Captain Nicholas, it seemed. Perry then asked him if he remembered if he recollected the time when Knapp's and Waldy's bedclothes had been thrown out of the window into the barrack square? Llewellyn remembered Knapp's being thrown out, but not Waldy's. He had been present himself, and so had Dallas. He did not remember who the other officers were. The court asked if Captain Nicholas had been involved in this incident? He had not. Llewellyn had never himself been the subject of practical jokes. He had not been present when an officer had been reprimanded by Colonel Garrett for annoying Perry. He thought Perry was not generally shunned by his brother officers but his company was not much sought after, on account of his disagreeable manner. He did not know of any letter written by Perry to Colonel Garrett threatening to report to the general of the district. He did not agree that upwards of six officers took part in the Waldy affair, and remembered only himself. Perry pressed him. Would he say that only he and Dallas were present when Waldy's bedclothes were thrown out, his bed taken to pieces, everything in the room tossed about, and in Knapp's room, his bedclothes thrown out of the window, boots filled with water, everything thrown about, and his bedstead taken to pieces? Was it possible that he and Dallas could have done this alone? Llewellyn thought that there were other officers in Waldy's room but he forgot who they were. At 4 o'clock the court adjourned.

The tenth day

On Tuesday, 8th August, the court met again for its tenth day of hearing. *The Times* noted that 'the anxiety of the public to witness the proceedings was intense and every accomodation consistent with the limited dimensions of the court and the regularity of the proceedings was courteously afforded by the president'. Among those present during the day were Sir John Cathcart of Cooper's Hill, Colonel Craufurd, Grenadier Guards, Colonel the Hon Cecil Forster, Royal Horse Guards (Blue), two county magistrates and the Mayor of Windsor, Mr JT Bedborough. Mr Darvill of Windsor was present as the prisoner's adviser.

Lieutenant Alfred Henry Waldy, the elder brother of WT Waldy who had already given evidence, was sworn. He had been in the regiment since 14 December 1849. Captain Nicholas's impeccable behaviour to new officers was again described. Perry then directed him towards more specific details. Waldy Senior remembered a night when the officers of the 21st Regiment had dined with the 46th. He had not seen Perry coming to the mess room in uniform to report to Colonel Garrett the indignities to which he had been subjected. He did not go to Perry's room that night to ask him not to report the offenders, including Lieutenant Curtis, to the district general. He had not the slightest recollection of ever going to Perry's room to ask him not to report anyone. To the court's questions he did not remember exactly when the dinner concerned took place, he thought it must have been July 1853; he had not been present when Colonel Garrett reprimanded an officer for annoying Lieutenant Perry; he knew of no indignities received by Perry for having complained. He thought that Perry's company was avoided in consequence of his disagreeable forward manner. The court asked if Lieutenant Curtis had come to his room on receiving three questions to answer from Colonel Garrett? Waldy said that he had not been there, but his brother had told him of the call. He was stood down, and Lieutenant John Augustus Fane was called and sworn. The usual glowing character reference for Nicholas was given. Perry asked if he had seen in the newspapers what previous witnesses had said. He had. Of other relevant matters he knew nothing, or had forgotten. He thought Perry's society was avoided by other officers for his general overbearing and swaggering manner.

Greer

Greer, still under arrest, was called and sworn. He had been confined to his room and not allowed to walk in the Barrack-square for 38 days and this appeared to have materially affected his health. He had been in the regiment for five years and two months. He shared his brother officers' opinion of Captain Nicholas' fine character and kindness to new officers. The prisoner asked if he had said to Lieutenant Shervinton, the night before that officer left for Turkey, that Perry had been an ill-treated and badly used man ever since he had joined the regiment. He had no recollection of this, nor was he aware that Shervinton had later gone to Perry's room to pass on Greer's good feeling towards Perry. Perry protested that Greer must remember what had happened only three weeks before, but the court said he had answered the question. Perry now asked if Greer had been reading the papers, and discussing the nature of the evidence with other officers. Greer said he had, with one or two of the six or seven officers who had been with him (as escorts during his arrest, presumably), but the only name he could remember was Coote's. This was because he had had more discussion with him. Perry pressed for the names of the others. Without them it was impossible for him to defend himself. Every witness could shield himself in that way and the truth could never be elicited. The President commented that it would be all in Perry's favour, and the court considered Perry's request for the names. It made no order, and Perry said that if the witness was to refuse to answer his questions, then he would ask no more. The court asked Greer about the Shervinton incident. Greer remembered no message to Perry. The prisoner changed his mind and asked more questions, but Greer had never heard Colonel Garrett reprimand Perry for reporting and call him a 'fool for his pains'. He knew of no indignities suffered by Perry for this.

The Adjutant speaks

The adjutant, Lieutenant M'Alister, was called. He had been in the regiment since July 1847 when he joined the depot, then in Guernsey. Captain Nicholas's character was again praised. Perry asked about pressure on him from Colonel Garrett to sell out. M'Alister denied pressure but agreed that the colonel had advised him to. Perry asked specifically if the colonel had said that he had spoken to one of the authorities at Horse Guards who had agreed that Perry had no chance and had better sell out. The witness appealed that as adjutant he should not be called upon to report the colonel's words to him. Perry said that as he himself had been present it could not therefore be confidential, but if M'Alister refused he would not press it. The court conferred and asked M'Alister under what circumstances Perry had been advised to sell out. It had been after an assault committed by him on Greer, who had also been advised to do the same. Lieutenant Hesketh was re-called. He had been in the 46th for some six years. He gave the now familiar evidence of Captain Nicholas's fine qualities.

Campbell's high moral tone

The court adjourned for ten minutes and Captain Campbell gave evidence. He had been in the regiment for nine years and knew Captain Nicholas well. He never annoyed young officers nor did he aid and abet others in doing so. Perry asked what period of the last two years Campbell had been with the regiment? All but the nine months he had spent on leave, was his answer. He had never known Nicholas join in a practical joke to annoy any

119

person. The court asked if Campbell knew that Perry's company had been shunned by his brother officers, and if so why had this been? Campbell said that he himself avoided Perry's company for his impertinent familiarity, his general depraved habits, a disgusting gesture he made towards a friend of Campbell's, and the general difficulty he had during the short time Perry was under command in keeping him within the bounds of discipline. Perry had been under command for about a month on detachment. He had one or two occasions to speak to Perry about his remissness; on another occasion Perry wrote to him for an extension of leave, but took it before he had received Campbell's answer. For this Campbell publicly reprimanded him before all the officers, stopped all his future leave and threatened him with arrest. The Court asked about his depraved habits. Campbell knew of these only from what brother officers had told him. It seemed that he kept the company of prostitutes. Perry had also treated military discipline with contempt. When in Manchester, the acting adjutant had reported that he had been gravely insulted. He had handed an official memorandum to Perry who had made a gesture of wiping his posterior with it, and had then handed it back. Campbell had told the acting adjutant to report this at once to Major Fyffe. Perry asked if he could leave the court to get the letters referring to this incident. The President said that they could be presented during Perry's defence. Campbell had never heard the colonel reprimand Perry and call him a fool for his pains, nor had he heard that Perry had threatened to complain to the general until he had read it in the report of Greer's trial in the newspapers. Perry asked Campbell if he had himself been in the company of prostitutes, and if most of the officers of the regiment were not addicted to their company. Campbell admitted that he had himself been in their company, but denied that the officers were addicted to it. General Wetherall, the prosecutor, intervened to say that incriminating others was no defence. Perry said he was sorry that irrelevant matter had been introduced, and hearsay evidence received, and he would have to contradict it and bring far more disgusting matters before the Court in self-defence. He had tried to keep irrelevant matter out of the trial but, if it is thrust in, as it had been by the witness, he must meet it. He was prepared to disprove and explain all that had been gratuitously put forward by Campbell. The President said that the question did not bear upon the charge. Perry pointed out that Campbell had said it was the reason for avoiding his society and it showed the vindictiveness of the witness. The court was cleared for an hour.

The Deputy Judge Advocate then ruled that, having looked into the highest authorities, the law protected a witness from incriminating himself, and if a question did not bear directly upon the charge he could decline to answer. If the question was essential to the proof of the charge, or the defence of the accused, the witness must give the best answer he could. The court had allowed the prisoner every indulgence and had allowed him to cross-examine without limit or restraint, but bearing in mind the evil results of personal recrimination, they had decided that the question could not be put. Perry humbly requested the Court to read the letters concerned and to place them on the record. The Deputy Judge Advocate said that this could be done during Perry's defence, but for the moment a witness was being cross-examined. Perry asked for a written protest to be entered on the record. The President said that the court must finish with the witness first. Perry asked what was the result of the disgusting gesture affair? Campbell said the case was reported to Major Fyffe, and letters were written by Shervinton, the acting adjutant involved, Perry and then Shervinton again. Shervinton had finally agreed to treat the matter as a jest and not as a breach of discipline. He thought the adjutant had the letters now. Perry said he was anxious that the letters be now read as the accusation of him would go forth in the public journals the next morning. Captain Pechell, a member of the court, said that they had nothing to do with the public journals. Wetherall said he had now finished the prosecution case and suggested that Perry reserve the letters for his defence. Perry agreed and the court adjourned after four o'clock.

The eleventh day

The eleventh day, Wednesday 9th August, the court-room was again densely crowded as the proceedings were resumed. Captain Campbell was about to be examined, when Perry asked that the last question and answer the preceding day be read. They were about the letters relating to the incident in Manchester and the answer had been that they were with the adjutant. Perry asked that they be produced. The Deputy Judge Advocate said that he must go on with his cross-examination, and for the moment the letters were not before the court in any tangible shape. Perry asked if the prosecutor would produce them as Perry needed them for his defence. General Wetherall said that if there was any way he could he would do so with pleasure, but he knew nothing of them. The Deputy Judge Advocate said that Perry could call Colonel Garrett, or the Adjutant, or any one else, when the cross-examination of Campbell was completed, but once finished he could not be recalled. Perry then read the following protest: 'I must respectfully protest against not being allowed fully to cross-examine the witness. The difficulty I am thereby placed in is this - that I am not enabled to impeach the testimony of a witness out of his own mouth, but am told that I may call witnesses in my defence to do so; which I respectfully submit is opposed to the principles and law of evidence, and places me in a most painful and difficult position, because in examination-in-chief I could not be allowed to put the same searching questions as I am justified and entitled to do in cross-examination.' General Wetherall said that if the Court thought it regular he would call for the letters.

Letters are produced

On advice from the Deputy Judge Advocate, the Court agreed and the Adjutant M'Alister was called and produced the letters. The court was cleared and on resumption the Deputy Judge Advocate read them as follows:

'Major Fyffe to Colonel Garrett, Weedon May 31,
To Lieutenant Colonel Garrett, KH, Commanding 46th Regiment.
Sir, I have the honour to report that I have been compelled to place Lieutenant Perry and Ensign Knapp in arrest, for repeated neglect of duty and contempt of authority. The enclosed letter from Lieutenant Shervinton, upon whom I called for a statement of the instances of neglect, &c, against the abovenamed officers will explain the circumstances of the case, and I have only to add that repeated reprimands and admonitions having failed in producing any effect I am most reluctantly obliged to adopt the step I have taken, and to refer the matter to you for your consideration.
I have the honour to be, Sir, your obedient servant,
David Fyffe, Major, Commanding Division, 46th Regiment'

'Lieutenant Shervinton to Major Fyffe, Weedon May 31,
To the officer commanding 46th Regiment, Weedon.
Sir, In obedience to your orders, I beg to state below some of the complaints against Lieutenant Perry and Ensign Knapp, which I have found necessary at various times to bring to your notice.
Lieutenant Perry some short time ago (in the presence of Ensign Waldy and his servant), upon the occasion of my handing him a memorandum respecting drills, which were written by your directions, went through the motions of wiping his posteriors with it and returned it to me.

He has also been absent as well as late for drills. On the 25th inst he was absent from afternoon drill for which omission he was directed by you to attend morning drills until further orders.

Ensign Knapp I have had to bring before you for absence from morning drill; also for sulkiness and general inattention on several occasions; together with improper conduct during divine service (reported by Captain Clarke). Having been reported absent from a board which assembled on Saturday last, he was directed by you to attend morning drills until further orders.

Lieutenant Perry and Ensign Knapp thus attending morning drill for omissions of duty were reported to me this morning by the sergeant major for dictating and ordering him to substitute company drill for the position drill named in orders. The question having been settled by reference to me, they, after a considerable lapse of time, fell into the ranks in a most discontented and unofficer-like manner, which (I understand) caused considerable merriment to the men.

The position drill (which they consider derogatory to their rank and position in the service) consisted of the extension motions and the usual portions of the sword exercise.

I have the honour to be, Sir, your obedient servant,

C.R. Shervinton, Lieutenant 46th Regiment, Acting Adjutant Detachment'

There was an enclosed document:

'Memorandum, Manchester May 9, 1854 - The following officers will attend morning drill at 7 a.m. until further notice: Lieutenant Perry, Ensign Knapp, Ensign Waldy, Ensign Hulton,

By order, C.R. Shervinton, Lieutenant and Adjutant, Detachment 46th Regiment.'

The Commanding Officer's reply

Colonel Garrett's reply to Major Fyffe was dated from Windsor on June 1st. He wrote: 'Judging of Lieutenant Perry by his antecedents, I am not surprised by what has occurred, but I had hoped that Ensign Knapp, although not an officer of much promise, might by attention have improved, and advanced in the service without animadversion.

The conduct of Lieutenant Perry has been in gross violation of discipline and insolent contempt of your authority, and in my opinion, can only be disposed of by being brought before the cognizance of a court-martial. I may possibly feel it to be my duty to institute the same line of proceeding in Ensign Knapp's case, in order to enforce the discipline of the service, which he, as well as Lieutenant Perry, has set at naught. At all events I have no doubt that I shall be under the necessity of recommending that his expected promotion do not take place.

I will call on Ensign Waldy and his servant tomorrow for a summary of the evidences as to the insolent contempt of authority shown by Lieutenant Perry, as reported by you, and I shall thereon frame charges against him, and forward them to you, in order that he may offer any observations regarding them if he can, previously to submitting them to the General Commanding-in-Chief. Both these officers will remain in arrest until their cases have been disposed of.'

The charges framed by Colonel Garrett and forwarded to Major Fyffe were as follows:

'Charges against Lieutenant Perry:

First, for conduct unbecoming the character of an officer in having at Manchester, on or about .... May 1854, on receiving from Lieutenant and Acting Adjutant Charles Shervinton, a memorandum containing certain orders from Major Fyffe, then commanding the division of the 46th Regiment at Weedon, treated that document by certain signs and motions in a most ignominious and contemptuous manner.

Second, For wilfully absenting himself from parades on or about the 25th of May, 1854.

The whole of such conduct being in contempt of the authority of his commanding officer, and subversive of good order and military discipline.

R. Garrett, Lieutenant Colonel, Commanding 46th Regiment.'

There was also a note from Garrett to Fyffe detailing the items of evidence which would be needed to deal with Knapp's case:

Summary of his absence from parade, or morning drill, and date thereof.

Also for sulkiness and inattention at various drills, and their dates.

Also misconduct at divine service and date.

Also as to absence from a regimental board, on or about the 27th of May.

Also full particulars and summary of evidence as to the misconduct of Lieutenant Perry and Ensign Knapp, at morning parade, on or about the 21st of May, when for drill.

Whether the Adjutant was present when these officers ordered the sergeant major to depart from the written orders regulating that parade.

Also a summary of various evidences as to their conduct after reprimand to the acting adjutant on the above subject.'

Perry apologizes

A letter from Perry to the colonel followed:

'To the Officer Commanding 46th Regiment, Windsor

Sir, In reply to the charges preferred against me, I have the honour to state, with regard to the first, I was in Ensign Waldey's room, and in a high flow of spirits, when Lieutenant and Acting Adjutant

C. Shervinton came in and handed me a memorandum, which having read, I returned him, but, unfortunately, forgot the respect due to him as the representative of the commanding officer, and in a moment of excitement (caused by what had taken place previous to his entrance) I committed an offence which in cooler moments I never would have been guilty of, and for which I afterwards made such an apology as appeared sufficient to Major Fyffe, and also satisfactory to Lieutenant and Acting Adjutant C. Shervinton.

I may mention, in further extenuation, that I had previously been on terms of great intimacy and familiarity with Lieutenant Shervinton, and that what I did was merely meant as a joke; and I have no doubt that he would have taken it as such had it not been for the official nature of his communication.

I have the honour to state, with regard to the second charge, that I was orderly officer on the 25th of May, 1854. I visited the hospital between 2 o'clock and half past 2 (which latter was the drill hour), in hopes of being in time for drill, which I would have done had I not been detained at the hospital for several minutes, there being no orderly there to show me round the wards. I afterwards turned out the magazine guard, and visited the sentries. When I arrived in the barrack square, by the back gate, the men had fallen in and were drilling under the sergeant major. Seeing I was late, I did not like to fall in for fear of disturbing the parade. I then performed my duties as orderly-officer by turning out the barrack gate guard, visiting the sentries, canteen, &c.

I have nothing further to state in my defence, but throw myself on the generosity of my commanding officer, trusting that through your clemency I may yet have an opportunity of showing my sincere regret for the past, and by my future conduct of proving myself worthy of the leniency extended to me; and I hope you may be induced to look upon the first and more serious charge in its true light, of an unthinking boyish trick, and not in any way intended as an insult to established authority.

I am now quite aware of the very serious consequences entailed by such an improper action.

Hoping that you will extend your mercy and not enforce the serious measures you appear to have in contemplation.

I have the honour to be, Sir, your obedient humble servant, J.F. Perry, Lieutenant 46th Regt.'

Garrett is not satisfied

There followed a memorandum dated June 6th from Colonel Garrett to Major Fyffe, saying that Perry's letter was not satisfactory as regards the contempt shown to Fyffe's authority, nor as regards his absence from parade on May 25th. It continued: 'The contempt shown by him was in the presence of a private of the regiment; and the impression in the mind of the commanding officer is that it was designed, wilful and premeditated. The offence however consists in the *animus* under which it took place, and the commanding officer must be satisfied by other statements than those of Lieutenant Perry that it was an unintentional and thoughtless oversight. Lieutenant Perry's acts are a tissue of opposition to the authority of his commanding officer, and cannot be allowed to pass. He has stated his wish to serve elsewhere, but the commanding officer cannot give any opinion as to his so doing, and thus escaping an ordeal which his conduct asks for, until he has shown by other statements than his own that his acts were the result of thoughtfulness and inadvertence.'

This was no doubt passed on by Major Fyffe to Perry for he then produced a letter from Shervinton, dated Weedon June 7th. It was clearly a reply to one from Perry of the same date, in which Perry had called on Shervinton to state his beliefs as to Perry's intention (or otherwise) to show contempt or disrespect for Major Fyffe by his treatment of an official document from him. Shervinton wrote that he was still of the same opinion as when he had reported the incident: he thought that he had acted in a thoughtless and inconsiderate manner, without the most distant intention of showing contempt for authority, or committing a breach of discipline. Perry, no doubt with relief, passed this at once to Major Fyffe, with a covering note, and this was forwarded to Colonel Garrett the same day.

Garrett reluctantly forgives

The next day the colonel replied to Major Fyffe, stating that the tenour(sic) of Perry's letter had not persuaded him that the offence had been of thoughtlessness, or that he had not been in wilful contempt of the major, but he was disposed to give Perry the benefit of the doubt which perhaps existed in other's minds, but certainly not in his. If Major Fyffe was satisfied not to allow it to go before the authorities, then he might, in the presence of the subalterns, admonish Perry and caution him against the repetition of such unofficerlike and improper conduct, and also on the danger of absenting himself from his duties, and misconduct while at drill on parade. Fyffe was to admonish Ensign Knapp at the same time and both were to be warned to be very circumspect in future, and not to expect any indulgences or other consideration until their future conduct induced the commanding officer to consider that they deserved it. Meanwhile both officers were to be released from arrest and to return to duty.

Major Fyffe was then recalled by the court and formally identified the letters. Perry asked to see the letter to him from Shervinton and Captain Campbell was recalled. Perry put it to him that in his evidence he had said that Lieutenant Shervinton 'consented' to consider the matter as a jest, and not as a breach of military discipline, whereas his letter showed that he made no compromise of the kind, but thought Perry had acted in a thoughtless and inconsiderate manner, without the most distant

129

intention of showing contempt for military authority, or committing a breach of discipline. Campbell replied that from the excited state of Shervinton when he had first gone to Campbell's room to report the incident he could not imagine that at that time he had taken it as a jest, or otherwise than as a deliberate insult. He had not been present when Shervinton had reported it to Major Fyffe, nor had he seen any letters except one from Shervinton in which that officer, to the best of Campbell's belief, had said that he was willing to consider that Perry had acted in a thoughtless and inconsiderate manner, without the most distant intention of committing a breach of military discipline. The actual Shervinton letter was shown to Captain Campbell who read it attentively, but made no comment.

Perry objects to the letters

Perry then handed in a written protest against the letters being included in the record of the trial except those which bore directly on the charges. He wanted his letter and Lieutenant Shervinton's reply before the court, so that he could cross-examine Campbell on them, and he protested against the other letters being received or entered upon the minutes. The court was cleared, and on re-assembly the Deputy-Judge Advocate said that they had received a protest from Perry, but could neither receive it, entertain it, or recognise it in any way. They admit no protest against their proceedings. He handed it back to Perry. (The decision was later amplified that all the letters referred to one transaction and that the whole or none of them should be read. In the event all were read and entered in the minutes.)

Perry resumed questioning of Captain Campbell. Campbell adhered to his previous evidence about Shervinton's attitude. Perry now asked him what he meant by impertinent familiarity, and Campbell said it was addressing him by his Christian name.

Perry said that he had called him this - 'Colin' - once when they were dining with other officers, and was he not generally called Colin by other officers? Campbell said that when Perry had used his Christian name he had told him not to. He was generally called Colin by other captains, and by some lieutenants. He agreed that Perry had not done this since. The prosecution case was then closed and Perry asked for an adjournment until Monday 14th August in order to prepare his defence. This was granted.

Support for the establishment

The Times of Thursday the 10th of August brought a report of the above proceedings, likely to please supporters of the Horse Guards, Colonel Garrett and the 46th generally, and there was also a firm rebuttal of the charges contained in the letter from 'A civilian' which had been printed on the 7th. Officers who sat on courts-martial did not take their oaths lightly. Courts of Inquiry were not packed with sympathetic officers by Horse Guards, who played no part in selecting members in most such Inquiries. They were composed of the battalion major and two of its senior captains. The aristocrats who joined the army did *not* join hoping not to see active service and the Duke of Wellington had testified that they had stood hardships as well as anyone. Considering a regiment as a type of club was fair, but that was why, the writer thought, our army was superior in the quality of its officers to any other. He did think that it would be better if the possession of private means by candidates for commissions was formally required as an ensign's pay of 5s 3d (about 27p) a day could not possibly maintain an officer in any regiment in the service. Any candidate who showed signs of mental or bodily weakness should not be in the army where it would lead to ruin, and endanger his men's lives. And it was absurd to suggest that the Horse Guards did not take very seriously complaints of behaviour such as revealed in the present case. Only last year they had dismissed from the service officers of the 50th Regiment of the most aristocratic and influential families for using language of which those afterwards attending a large meeting of the Army and Navy Club had admitted nobody present was guiltless. The correspondent, identified only as 'W.B', was clear that the published evidence would not bear out the charge made by the earlier writer against Colonel Garrett.

A witty comment

The next day's newspaper had, of course, no report of proceedings, but two letters on the subject. One was from a medical doctor, who had noted the complete and sudden loss of memory which had afflicted the officers of the 46th. He had studied the medical literature, but could find no parallel. Individual cases were not unknown, including a certain German statesman who had asked a friend who he himself was as he had forgotten. The leading authority described four varieties of this mental imbecility: stupidity, amnesia, credulity and inconstantia or fickleness. He did not think that stupidity was the problem, but amnesia seemed to have spread from the colonel down with all the virulence of a severe epidemy. It needed a careful investigation from the regimental surgeon, and it would not be safe to allow the regiment to embark for the east with so many invalid officers. He was also concerned in case the members of the court became victims to the third type of the disease: credulity.

The other letter was apparently from a lawyer, and was extremely critical of 'W.B's letter, mentioned above, and of the legal shortcomings of the courts-martial and procedures. W.B. was mistaken in thinking that it was proper for the prosecutor to go into evidence incriminating or damaging the accused, and then to interfere and prevent the accused cross-examining upon such evidence, whether thought to be irrelevant or not. The court had no power to compel the unfortunate man to go into evidence in chief if he thought that he could get at the exculpatory matter better by way of cross-examination. It exceeded its proper authority when it would not allow him to impeach the credit of Captain Campbell, who had accused him, and had spoken of the regimental horror of prostitutes. Nor had it the right to force the accused to call Colonel Garrett, Captain Campbell or any other witness hostile to him, to give evidence for him, thereby putting himself in the exceedingly painful position of having every word of theirs taken strongly against him, whereas every word of theirs given in cross-examination would have been taken against the prosecutor. W.B. had also drawn attention to the fact that the present prosecutor was the Adjutant-General of the army and had been sent down on that duty by the Horse Guards, the Horse Guards thus being committed against Perry before they had given their impartial judgement in the first two courts-martial, not to mention their duty to be impartial in considering the verdict of the present court-martial when it was finished. Further, Greer, the subject of one of the two first courts-martial, was produced as a witness against Perry. Finally, the writer drew attention to the fact that a member of one of the first two courts-martial, the commanding officer of one of the household regiments, had after weeks of difficulty been able to solve with a Court of Inquiry a matter which must have otherwise gone to court-martial, giving publicity to a state of affairs in one of Her Majesty's Regiments of guards, scarcely if at all inferior in scandal to that of the 46th Foot...

Chapter 7 - The decision in the first court-martial of Lieutenant Perry

The issue of 11th August also contained an important item of news datelined Windsor, Thursday night. It reported that that morning an express arrived from the Horse Guards bearing a despatch announcing the final decision in the first court-martial of Perry on the charge of assaulting Lieutenant Greer. It had been read to the officers of the 46th that morning, and passed to Perry at about midday. Colonel Garrett had declined to tell the reporter of *The Times* of the result, and Lieutenant Perry had been away all day at the residence of his solicitor, Mr Darvill.

The court-martial had found Perry guilty of the charge and had sentenced him to be dismissed from the service, but unanimously recommended him to mercy on account of the great provocation he had received. The Judge Advocate General had, however, found that certain questions had been put which ought to have been rejected, and certain evidence refused which ought to have been taken, and he recommended Her Majesty not to confirm the sentence. Accordingly it was not confirmed, and Lieutenant Perry was released from that charge. *The full decision is given at Appendix D.*

Greer's decision near, Perry's friends confident

On 10th August, on application of his solicitor, Lieutenant Greer had been released from arrest on his parole of honour. A decision in his case was expected any day. Meanwhile it was noted that the friends of Perry were confident that they could prove the whole of the charges contained in the letter to Colonel Upton, as well as those in his evidence and letter to Colonel Pipon about Captain Nicholas. They looked forward to bringing his defence with great interest.

More criticism of 'W.B.'

The Times of 15 August contained another letter critical of that from 'W.B.' A writer identified as 'A Civilian' first approved of what 'A.' had said in rebuttal, and then went on to point out that some criticism of Perry in other newspapers had been very unfair. Perry was a youth with no near relations or friends in a position to assist him. He was also poor and had had to consult a lawyer to guide him in the conduct of his defence. But the method of conducting the trial meant that although the lawyer advised him on what questions to put, it always appeared that they were directly from Perry himself. His legal adviser was evidently a very clever fellow and had seen the incompetence, ignorance and partiality of the first tribunal, and through Perry as mouthpiece had made those shortcomings so apparent that the Horse Guards could not advise Her Majesty to confirm the absurd and unjust sentence which the tribunal had passed. Some sections of the press had then rounded on Perry for being a regular lawyer, for conducting his defence so well and exposing the apathy and negligence of his colonel. No wonder, they had deduced, that his brother officers did not like him!

His legal adviser had brought out the facts that his colonel had neglected his duty, his brother officers professed to dislike him for his familiarity and immorality but were in every respect far more culpable than the man they were conspiring to ruin. It was fortunate that Perry had had such a good effective lawyer and, although he would probably be ruined by the bill, the lawyer had served him well. He turned to the evidence of Captain Colin Campbell, regretting that he had to write anything against the bearer of a name so justly loved and respected in the British army, and ridiculed him for saying that he had refrained from Perry's company because he had called him by his Christian name - as so many other officers did - and as he 'had heard' that he associated with prostitutes, whereas under cross-examination when asked if he himself, and all of the other officers had also done so, he had admitted that it was so. Incidentally, the writer pointed out that when this question had been asked, the President had not sought to interfere, nor ought he to have done so, but General Wetherall of the Horse Guards, the prosecutor, did, warning Perry that incriminating others was not justification, and would do him no good. Yet despite this bullying by the representative of the Horse Guards, how right it was to ask the question was revealed by the answer, which impressed every impartial mind as to how worthless Campbell's evidence as to Perry's character was. What could one think of the evidence of a man who says he shuns the company of a youth for using his Christian name, thus revealing 'impertinent familiarity', yet who with his special friends was in the constant habit of dragging young strangers who had just joined the regiment violently out of their beds at 4 a.m., throwing their belongings out of the window, and bringing them down naked to the mess room to sing songs upon the table? This might appear to non-military readers to have a degree of 'impertinent familiarity' about it, yet Campbell seemed to find it far more objectionable to be addressed by his Christian name.

Perry's Defence

The papers of 15 August also carried what every one had eagerly awaited: Lieutenant Perry's defence to the new charges.

The first witness was his legal advisor, Mr Darvill, a solicitor. He explained the circumstances of the letter to Colonel Upton, signed by Perry. While Perry was preparing his defence to the charges in the trial of Lieutenant Greer, Mr O'Donovan, a legal friend of his who normally lives in Ireland, had pointed out that while Darvill had been absent from court (and O'Donovan had been temporarily acting as legal friend) the evidence of Major Maxwell and others amounted to a second trial of Perry and he had recommended that letters be sent to the court. Darvill had not been present during the evidence concerned so had relied on the judgement of his friend. They had gone with Perry to another's house, where Darvill had drawn up the letter and Perry had signed it. O'Donovan had taken the letter to the court and passed it in. A draft of it had been left on the table there, and this had somehow passed to the papers. Perry could not be morally answerable for the contents of the letter as he had merely signed it. The letter had been to the effect that if Perry had been allowed to cross-examine the witnesses he would have proved his case. And Darvill was confident that the truth of the letter would be proved. Wetherall asked who had written the letter, and if Perry had known of its contents when he had signed it. Darvill had written it, and though Perry knew of the nature of it, he did not know the particulars. The court asked about the third party present when the letter was prepared and signed. Darvill was reluctant to name him, but admitted that he was a reporter for the public papers.

Captain and Paymaster Corcoran was then sworn and examined. He had been 31 years in the service, had been with the 46th in the East Indies, in the West Indies, at Gibraltar, in Canada and at home. He was about to retire on half pay. He had been paymaster for about 13 years. Practical jokes had been common in the regiment for at least ten years. Within the last three years young officers had come to him for advice under the pressure of circumstances. They included Perry, Knapp, Dunscombe and

Lennard. Perry had come frequently in Dublin complaining of the nuisances to which he was subjected. The first four times Corcoran had advised him to bear it with patience and take it in good part. He did. Corcoran had pointed out that when officers junior to Perry joined they would have the same pranks played on them. The next time Perry had come and said that he had been forced to go through the sword exercises in his room, while naked and in the presence of officers from the 24th Regiment as well as his own. Corcoran had pointed out at page 115 of the *Queen's Regulations* his mode of redress. In the first place he ought to report the facts to one of the regiment's field officers. If that brought him no satisfaction he should report it officially to Colonel Garrett. The annoyance was still continued and Perry threatened to report it to the general of the district. Corcoran had advised him to write to Colonel Garrett and the following day Perry told him that at the solicitation of the other officers he had withdrawn the letter to the general, and if the persecution and annoyance ceased he would say nothing about it. As he seemed to feel the last attack so acutely Corcoran cautioned him never to join in any practical joke on a young officer. He tried to impress that on every young officer that he had spoken to. The next day Perry had told him that the colonel had said he was a fool for his pains, and was like a child just escaped from his mother's apron-strings. He was very much distressed and in tears. Corcoran had believed what Perry had said. He had advised him to apply to the general, and he thought that he had done so. After he had been the cause of another officer being reprimanded his society had been shunned by other officers. Corcoran had been told this but was married and lived a long way from the barracks so that he had not so good an opportunity of knowing, but he was sure of this and that it was because of his official complaint. Corcoran thought Perry particularly kind and obliging in his manner and he spent the greater part of his time when off duty playing the cornopean with another young officer. Corcoran could hear them daily. The prosecutor asked when the colonel had called Perry a fool for his pains. Corcoran thought it about the end of May 1853. He had no personal knowledge of this but thought another officer had told him. Similarly he only knew of the complaint to the general as Perry had told him of it. He did not think it likely that any other officer would have told him of this. Wetherall pressed him and he thought that Knapp did. Corcoran knew nothing of Captain Nicholas annoying Perry or any other young officers. Perry had not written the letter to Colonel Garrett threatening to report to the general in Corcoran's office. The officers who had persuaded Perry not to write to the general were Captain Nicholas and Lieutenant Curtis. Corcoran's only direct personal knowledge that practical jokes had been played was from seeing doors that had been smashed, and the water with which passages had been saturated, the previous night.

Corcoran was asked if anyone had spoken or written to him, to prepare him for what he was to say to the court martial. He had received three written questions, but as he was ready to tell the truth to this or any other court they had not influenced him at all. The questions were: was he prepared to attend the court-martial? Could he remember the date of the report by Perry to Garrett? And what was the name of any officer reprimanded by the colonel? Corcoran withdrew.

The next witness was Captain John Chambers of the 4th West York Militia, formerly of the 46th. He had been in the Dublin Barracks with Perry but had left the regiment on the 28th April, last. Practical jokes had been common in the regiment, and Perry had often been the subject of them. He remembered Lieutenant Curtis saying that he had such fun in drawing that d----d fellow Perry, and that he had made him go through the sword exercises with an umbrella. He remembered Curtis telling him that the colonel had told Perry he was a fool for his pains for reporting.

140

It was openly spoken of after dinner that Perry had been blackguarded by the colonel for reporting. He had heard that Perry had threatened to report to the general of the district. At 4 o'clock the court-martial adjourned to the next day.

The thirteenth day

On Tuesday the 15th of August, its thirteenth day, the court-martial resumed, but without Captain the Earl of Longford who was excused on medical certificate. Captain Chambers told the court about the ragging of Knapp, and the junior Waldy brother. In the Linen-hall Barracks in Dublin a group composed of Chambers himself, Captain Garrett (the colonel's son), Greer, Lennard and some others he could not remember. They had gone for the purpose of drawing[47] Knapp and Waldy. The latter's door was open so they had gone in, pulled down the bed, and thrown the bedding and bedclothes out of the window into the barrack-square. When the others had gone he had gone down and brought up the bedclothes. He had been very sorry. Waldy had returned to his room shortly afterwards and Chambers helped him to put his room in order. Waldy said he would report to the colonel and Chambers had advised him not to, but to take things quietly. He had asked who had done it but Chambers declined.

Perry asked if Captain Nicholas had not been one of the officers. Chambers said he had thought at one time that Nicholas had been present, but he did not now think he was. Perry pointed out that yesterday Chambers had told him privately that Nicholas was present. Why was he now altering that? Had he spoken to Nicholas? Chambers had, but had not mentioned the court-martial.

---

[47] Presumably a slang expression akin to dragging a badger or fox from his hole, meaning to provoke, or perhaps its meaning as 'to pull out of shape or out of place'. *The Oxford English Dictionary*.

Chambers had also spoken to several other officers about the court-martial, and about practical jokes. He thought he had said to Major Vesey and Captain Garrett that he thought Nicholas was there, but that he had no recollection that he was. He was now positive that Nicholas was not there. Perry asked him if he had changed his mind on this within the last 24 hours, and after consulting other officers? Chambers prevaricated: he thought he was present, but now he thought that he wasn't. He always had a doubt about it, and after thinking about it he did not recollect him doing anything, and he was now positive that he was not there. Incidentally Ford had told him that he was there, but Chambers had no recollection of that. He had not been present in the Royal Barracks, Dublin, when Major Maxwell had ordered an officer brought down from his bed. He knew nothing of Lieutenant Dunscombe's case. He thought that many of the regiment's officers were cool to Perry although he had always conducted himself to Chambers as a gentleman.

The court asked if he understood that Colonel Garrett had called Perry a fool for his pains. Chambers said that Curtis had told him this, he thought on some occasion when Perry had either reported to the general or had threatened to do so. He thought that the colonel had reprimanded some officer for annoying Perry but he was not present at any such reprimand. He thought it was about the month of May, 1853, but he did not know who the officer was. No one had heard Curtis telling him about the colonel calling Perry a fool for his pains.

The Deputy Judge Advocate's offer of advice

He was stood down and Major Pack was called and sworn. He had been the Deputy Judge-Advocate in Perry's first trial. On the 12th of July (the first day of that trial) he had called in on

142

Perry in his room and had told him that he could ask any questions of Pack which he wished, as Pack was as much his adviser as the Court's. He had said as much in open court on the 14th. He was shown the letter Perry had sent to Colonel Pipon, and asked if he would have considered it privileged and would have returned it to Perry if he had not ordered it to be read to the court? Pack said he would have sent it to the President and would have asked the President to call Captain Nicholas. But he was not acting in that case.

Perry now wished to know the parade state of the different companies of the regiment the day before the two companies left for Portsmouth, en route to the East. The adjutant was recalled and went to the orderly room for the documents. They were to be produced the next day and Perry now asked that a letter from Lieutenant W.T. Waldy[48] be read to the court and it was. It was to Perry and was dated 12 June. Waldy understood that Perry wished to exchange to another regiment. Waldy considered the Windsor quarters 'very jolly'. There were lots of women but life was irksome. He had a good mind to exchange himself as he was pretty well tired of the South Devon. Nicholas had told Coote in the Mess that he was 'a d------d son of a bitch of an Ensign. The letter was signed by Waldy. He confirmed that it was in his handwriting. The Prosecutor asked how Waldy had known of the terms used by Nicholas to Coote described in the letter. Waldy could not remember. He did not think Nicholas was present but he did not know who had used the language. The Court asked him to explain the difference between what he was now saying, and the evidence he had given earlier in the trial. Waldy could not see the difference but pressed by the President accepted that there was a discrepancy but did not know what to add. He had written without

---

[48] There were two Waldy brothers in the regiment, Lieutenants Alfred Henry and William Thomas.

thinking. Colonel Blyth asked pointedly if that applied to the whole of his evidence. The witness was excused.[49]

The fourteenth day

The next day, the fourteenth day of the trial, began with Major Stuart, late of the 46th, being called and sworn. He agreed with the prisoner that practical jokes were common in the regiment and thought that they were encouraged. He believed that Major Maxwell had sent officers to bring down officers from their beds to the anteroom. He did not think that an officer reporting a brother officer to the commanding officer would receive redress. He had mentioned one case to the colonel and it had been received with apparent indifference and had been quite ineffectual. He had never observed Perry's manner to be overbearing and swaggering, and had thought his conduct regular and correct. According to Her Majesty's Regulations detachments sent overseas should be from

---

[49] Waldy did not know, but he was in grave danger of being court-martialled himself for his behaviour. A formal Court of Enquiry was held into the assertions he had made in his letter and when the Military Secretary at Horse Guards, Major General Yorke, saw the minutes of that enquiry on 24 August he passed the papers to the Deputy Judge Advocate General, S.C. Denison, Esq, for an opinion as to whether the evidence taken by that enquiry was sufficient to found charges against Waldy for his conduct in making such assertions, with a reasonable prospect of obtaining a conviction by a General Court Martial. Fortunately for Waldy, Denison did not think the evidence warranted his arraignment and thought it would be sufficient if Waldy apologised to Coote and Nicholas and, if Viscount Hardinge thought it expedient to do so, the latter issuing a reprimand. This, we shall see later, is what was done, and the prospect of a fourth court martial was avoided. Denison's letter to Yorke is at Appendix ?

the senior company downwards. He knew nothing of Perry being reproached, nor called a fool, nor of threats by Perry to appeal to the general. He did not know about Perry being subject to annoyance after complaining to the colonel and the particular incident of the ineffectual complaint had been in 1842. The Prosecutor complained that we might just as well go back to Waterloo.

Perry now referred to the parade states asked for the previous day, but had been told that the very one he wished to see had been destroyed. The other returns were of no relevance but he wished to say that Captain Hardy and Lieutenant Shervinton should not have gone to Turkey.

Perry's servant, Private Lawler was the next witness. He remembered taking a letter from Perry to Captain Campbell and that Campbell, M'Alister and Shervinton dined in a separate private mess in Shervinton's room. Perry never dined there. He told the court that Perry's room had been broken open, the lock torn off, his candles thrown on the floor, his clothing torn and all his things knocked about. Neither Court nor Prosecutor asked any questions. Lieutenant Lennard, late of the 46th was called but was not present. A medical certificate said he could not come because of diarrhoea. Perry addressed the court and said that Lennard was too ill to attend, Ensign Stretton was in the Turkish service, and Captains O'Toole and Hardy, Lieutenants Shervinton and Knapp, all witnesses material to his defence, had been sent to Turkey. They would greatly strengthen his defence but he would have to proceed without them. The court sat with closed doors for two hours and then adjourned to the following day.

Perry's Defence statement

On August 17th, the fifteenth day of his second trial, Lieutenant Perry gave his defence to a hushed courtroom, as follows: 'I have neither the means nor the intention to prolong this inquiry. I put in evidence the parade states of the companies, except the one most important to my case which is said to have been destroyed. And I put in the certified record of my evidence given on 21st July.' He then began to read a lengthy statement (the full text is at Appendix A) clearly prepared for him by his solicitor, Mr Davill. Its substance was as follows.

It was clear that the officers of the regiment had been called together and told what to say against him. The evidence had been 'prearranged' and answers were given in the same stereotyped phraseology. There had been a denial of such a gathering, and when it became clear that a meeting had taken place lasting an hour it was claimed that it was to discuss the mess accounts. Lieutenant Hesketh had however said that the officers were assembled to discuss the case and that meeting was not to audit the accounts. Perry as a young officer, without a father or relative to advise him, had his private character attacked and had been surrounded by conspiracy, combination, calumny and perjury. Time after time, when witnesses were asked pertinent questions they had said that they could not remember.

The four charges related broadly to two separate matters. He was charged with alleging that when he had complained to Colonel Garrett of being bullied, he had been called a 'fool for his pains' when this was not true. It was also alleged that he had falsely stated that he had threatened the colonel that he would complain to the General of the district. Garrett had apparently no memory of any such events and a procession of witnesses - all officers in Garrett's regiment and beholden to him as commanding

146

officer - had denied any knowledge of them. Nevertheless several of them had faltered in cross-examination and Chambers, no longer in the regiment, had corroborated Perry's statements. Corcoran, the Paymaster, had also clearly remembered the events. In any case, no quantity of *'non mi recordo'* ('I don't remember') evidence can amount to proof.

The second pair of charges involved Captain Nicholas: Perry had falsely stated in Greer's trial that Nicholas had ill-treated officers on joining, and Perry had written this in a letter to Colonel Pipon, Deputy Judge Advocate in that trial. Sixteen witnesses had been called, all testifying to Nicholas's fine character and exceptional kindness to young officers. It was eventually admitted that a meeting of the officers had been called to discuss the case and one, Waldy, had written in a letter of Nicholas's language to a young officer, an event of which he had denied knowledge in court.

The case had exhibited all the vindictiveness, preconcert and perjury of which he had complained in opening his defence. He solemnly declared that he was innocent of all the charges. At the conclusion of his address there was a loud cheer from the audience, which was speedily repressed by the Court. Major-General Wetherall commented that as he could not admit the truth of some of the statements made by the prisoner and the inferences drawn therefrom he must request that the Court be adjourned until half-past 1 o'clock to-morrow and this was done.

'The Times' criticises the trial

'The Times' accompanied its report of the proceedings on the 17th August with another blistering leading article. The 46th Regiment was clearly in such a condition that if almost all its officers were told that the Queen had no further need of their services it would be of little regret. All of the officers who had come to public notice, from the lieutenant colonel downwards, were either riotous, unmannerly schoolboys, or abettors of a vindictive and ungentlemanly combination against a young brother officer. Further, the prosecutor had behaved improperly. He had prevented the defence from cross-examining his witnesses and had obstructed their attempts to produce evidence of the state of the regiment. Finally, the witnesses needed by the defence had deliberately been sent out of the country before they could give evidence.

The newspaper could not complain about the verdict, nor the sentence, in Perry's first trial (which had now been quashed for irregular proceedings) but what a comment on Colonel Garrett that he had drawn no distinction between the luckless lad who had been assailed, and his brutal assailant. The proceedings had presented a sorry spectacle to the world and it was the commanding officer, not the subaltern, who stood condemned.

Greer's trial had been conducted virtually as a second trial of Perry, and the third trial, now in progress, had already shown the important shortcomings mentioned above. For example, Captain Campbell had testified that he had heard that Perry consorted with prostitutes, but there was no evidence of this and when questioned Campbell admitted that he himself did so. And witness after witness could not remember inconvenient facts. Waldy junior had stated that he had never heard or written anything against Captain Nicholas and was then shown his own letter doing just that. The leader writer suggested that the regiment's motto should be 'Non mi recordo' ('I can't remember'.) The newspaper's correspondence columns continued to receive a barrage of letters from readers, almost all condemning the behaviour of the 46th, and the treatment of Perry.

148

The Prosecutor replies

On the next day, Friday the 18th of August, the Prosecutor, Major General Wetherall, began his reply to Perry's defence. He thought the case simple. There were substantially three issues. When Perry had made a complaint to him, did Lieutenant Colonel Garrett reproach him and call him a fool for his pains? Did the prisoner send Garrett a letter threatening to complain to the commander of the district? And finally, was Captain Nicholas in the habit of ill-treating younger officers, or of aiding and abetting others in doing so? If these matters had not occurred, then Wetherall contended that the prisoner must have asserted what he knew to be false. He explained that if Garrett had prosecuted, as would be normal, then he would have been present throughout the trial, and as he was also a witness it had been decided that Wetherall would prosecute instead. Further, the normal procedure would have been simply to require Perry to prove his allegations, but in this case to assist him the prosecution had undertaken to try and prove the negative and Garrett and Nicholas had accepted this.

Now Garrett was clear that he had never said the words complained of. Major Maxwell who was present on the only occasion when it was likely to have happened had corroborated this, and no officer had even heard of it. On the second point, Garrett was adamant that he had received no such letter. Captain Sandwith, then the adjutant, was quite sure that there is and never has been such a letter in the orderly room. Again not one of the other officers had ever even heard of such a letter. Finally, a succession of officers had testified that they did not know of a single incident when Nicholas had ill-treated young officers and on the contrary their view of his character was that he could never have done so. That is the substance of the evidence for the prosecution. As for the defence witnesses, Mr Darvill was not able to prove any fact except that Perry had signed the letter he had drafted, but it was absurd to suggest that Perry thus escaped responsibility for its contents. Captain and Paymaster Corcoran knew nothing of events but what the accused had told him - hearsay of the least value. Captain Chambers' evidence was also hearsay.

At this point the defence introduced a letter signed by Lieutenant WT Waldy stating that Captain Nicholas had used an opprobious expression to Lieutenant Coote, but Coote himself had positively denied this and spoke, like the others, in the most gratifying terms of Captain Nicholas.

The fourth witness, Major Stewart, had personal knowledge only of an alleged incident fourteen years ago. The evidence of the fifth witness, Perry's servant Private Lawler, was irrelevant to the issues. Finally, Perry had alleged that witnesses who would have given evidence of assistance to him had been sent to Turkey to prevent that. Wetherall pointed out that the letter which gave rise to the trial had been written on 24th July, but all the officers sent to Turkey had been warned to go seven days earlier than that, on 17th July! Perry had said that he would prove the charges against Captain Nicholas but had not even attempted to substantiate those charges by producing any evidence at all. The case was left in the Court's hands. After deliberation for two hours they adjourned.

Chapter 8 More 'Thunder'

Once again, 'The Times' thundered in its leader. They had no hesitation in saying that in any ordinary court of justice the accused would be triumphantly acquitted. The evidence for the prosecution was in part worthless. The production of witnesses who had not heard Colonel Garrett call Perry a fool proved nothing. Nor did Garrett's own comment: 'I do not recollect ever having called Mr Perry a fool - I don't think I ever did' disprove the allegation, so clearly remembered and positively asserted by Perry. Later when asked if he had ever used reproachful language to any other officer who had been pulled out of bed, the colonel declined to answer. However, Paymaster Corcoran had given evidence that he had advised Perry to write to the general, and afterwards Perry said he had done so. He had also been told by Perry at the time that he had been called a fool by the colonel. Perry had come to him in tears after that incident. It was absurd to think that Perry had made up these facts a year before any prospect of any proceedings. Corcoran's evidence was also corroborated by another officer who remembered that the gentle rebuke given to Perry's tormentors had been the common talk of the regiment. If Colonel Garrett could not remember these facts then he had a very short memory indeed. The regiment under Garrett's control was in a most discreditable and disorderly condition. The officers' quarters were a veritable bear garden - every thing spoke of a vulgar riot. After his complaint Perry had become a tabooed man in the regiment, with every man's hand against him until at length he could bear it no longer and turned his hand in self defence against one. Hence the present proceedings.

As for Captain Nicholas, his non-production as a witness when he could have been cross-examined would in any civil court have at once disposed of the charge against Perry. But fortunately, there is positive evidence in Lieutenant Waldy's letter to show that Nicholas had called Ensign Coote 'a d-------d son of a b----h of an ensign'. This alone outweighs the evidence of the officers, who in any case had clearly been assembled to rehearse their evidence. One officer had claimed that the assembly had been to 'audit the mess accounts', but another had admitted that it was to discuss Perry's case. The testimony of these officers was tainted with the marks of vindictive combination. The whole trial was too disgusting and disgraceful and the officers of the 46th had lowered the public estimation of a British officer's character for many years to come. It was impossible not to see that great injustice has been done to Perry by the system of proceedings in these courts. May their decision, despite this, do justice to Perry, to maintain the character of the army and to give satisfaction to the public.

A fund to pay Perry's legal costs

The weekend now intervened and Monday's *Times* (August 21st) contained more letters of protest from the public, and one announcing the foundation of a fund to pay Perry's legal costs. Another quoted with approval the example of the 85th Regiment in 1810 under similar circumstances. The Duke of York, then Commander-in-Chief, had compelled every officer from the commanding officer down to exchange into other regiments, all in one day. Meanwhile for several days as the Court met in private to consider their decision, the *Times* continued to carry letters on the subject and to print its own angry comments.

A disgrace to the British Army

On Friday 25th August the newspaper commented on a number of those letters from the public and it agreed with virtually all of them. The prosecutions have been a disgrace to the British Army. There was even a rumour in Windsor that if Perry was acquitted - as he surely should be if there was one spark of justice left in the breasts of the military judges - he would be tried again for having charged the witnesses in this second trial with 'combination' and some with perjury. There would be no problem if such a trial was held before a competent tribunal and not before one of these courts-martial with its ridiculous idea of justice. If the likes of Fyffe, Campbell, Nicholas, Curtis and the Waldys, and above all Garrett himself, could be questioned by the Attorney-General, Sir Frederick Thesiger, before such a judge as Mr Justice Erle, or Mr Justice Cresswell, we might end by knowing something of the 46th. We should then know more of the behaviour of the officers of this corps in Ireland. It might appear that they are pre-eminently loose in their habits, and that Perry was not. This would explain why they have been against him but this - the key to the whole matter - will never be discovered by proceedings like those recently conducted at Windsor.

As they would not be familiar to most of the newspaper's readers, they set out the manner in which a court-martial operated. If the prisoner wished to cross examine a witness, he could not put it directly. He had to write it down on paper and the sergeant near him would pass it to the President who might raise a discussion on it in which all might join. Then it is passed to the Deputy Judge Advocate who reads it aloud, but not for the witness to answer as first he must write it down, and only then does he rise and put the question to the witness. Clearly any attempt by Perry to trip a witness, who he believed had discussed the evidence he would give, into contradiction, and to elicit the truth from him, was doomed. But worse, the Deputy Judge Advocate did not simply record the answer given but he allows the witness to alter and amend his evidence a dozen times before doing so. He helps a lame dog, as long as the dog is on the Prosecutor's side, over any awkward stile.

The Prosecutor's functions are even more anomalous. He frames his own questions and also stops questions from the prisoner in cross-examination. He makes and enforces his own rules and effectively performs all those duties which in a civil court would be done by judge, jury, defence counsel and prosecutor, and then finishes by telling the court how impartial he has been. What chance is there of a fair trial in a regiment where the real guilty party is the commanding officer himself? He enjoys unlimited powers to communicate with the witnesses whenever the court is cleared. He can hint to a friendly member of the court to ask a particular question, or to stop a troublesome witness, as Paymaster Corcoran was silenced. He and Nicholas had exchanged courtesies with the members of the court and Garrett had taken care to see that they had sandwiches and sherry whenever the court was adjourned or cleared. The Deputy Judge Advocate had taken quarters with the Horse Guards Blue, which had provided members to the various trials, and was friendly to them: it was said that in that regiment the same practices had taken place as in the 46th. Despite all this, the President, Colonel Kelly, appeared to be a high-minded man and might blunder into a right decision but was there ever such a way of arriving at the truth as a Court-martial? No wonder that the public, pre-eminently lovers of fair play - had been indignant at the proceedings. The previous day the newspaper noted that it had announced the foundation of a fund to discharge Perry's legal costs and this had never happened before in twenty years. *The Times* wished success to the fund, so disgraceful had been the persecution of Lieutenant Perry.

Over the next days letters continued to be sent to, and printed by, *The Times*. One in particular is worthy of note. A former commanding officer quoted from the Standing Orders he had issued to the regiment he had commanded:
'An important part of the duty of a commanding officer is to watch over the professional progress of the officers...(and) to watch over, with anxious care, the habits, dispositions, and general conduct of young officers, so as to ensure their undeviating pursuit of the path of strictest principle and honour; and never to permit in them gambling, dissipation, or extravagance.'

On the 29th August, the newspaper grumbled in a leader at the delay. It was now well into the second month since proceedings were first taken against Perry. Surely the Commander- in-Chief, Lord Hardinge, must realise that his decision must take into account all the circumstances of the case from first to last, and affected not just the individual but the character of the British army. He could either wash away the stain thrown upon the quality of a British officer by the conduct of the officers of the 46th Regiment or he would consign the upper ranks of the army to permanent contempt. If he did not mark his signal displeasure against those who have so foully abused their trust, the lofty pretension to treat an English officer and an English gentleman as synonomous was at an end. However courageous they might be they could not be considered as men of honour, honesty, humanity or integrity. They would be banished from the society of gentlemen and all women who regard the dignity and purity of their sex. Nor was it simply a matter of the 46th, disgusting though their behaviour had been, but of the taint that had spread throughout the English army. The public had not known that an English barracks could nightly be made a scene of bullying, riot, drunkenness and profligacy. A youth like Perry, who would not swim down the dirty stream with his fellows became marked for expulsion. It was to be hoped that in other regiments such testimony as had been given by the officers of the 46th would have been heard - surely things were not so bad as that - but in too many instances there was an equal amount of vice within the barrack walls.

As for the Perry case itself, it was an insult to any reasonable being to waste further comment. From the first court-martial it was clear that his conduct had been correct and it was singularly wrong for Lord Hardinge to have permitted him to be set up for a second time as a mark for the vulgar vengeance of his baffled assailants. The first trial had made clear that all the officers of the regiment, from the commanding officer downwards, were in a league against him. The second trial was in such a form that it was only necessary for his unmanly assailants to 'forget' to prove a negative case. It was significant that all the points which told against Perry were remembered but whenever an answer might have supported his case the never-failing answer was 'non mi recordo' *['I don't remember']*. In any case the issues were perfectly preposterous. There might have been reason to bring Colonel Garrett before a court-martial to answer for his general conduct in command of the regiment and there was grave suspicion against him. Instead, the young subaltern had been tried a second time. The writer was sick of the subject, but the English public must not get sick of it until full and ample justice had been done to Perry, not so much for his sake as for the reputation of the army. An adverse sentence would indelibly stain the character of every English officer from Lord Hardinge down, and even an acquittal, if accompanied by any words of censure would be an invitation to derision. If the military authorities were to continue to enjoy the confidence of the public, Perry should be reinstated in his former position.

Meanwhile, the tone and spirit of barrack life must be considered by the General Commanding-in-Chief. Is the mess room of a regiment to be a sort of taproom, and the officers' quarters a brothel? Is this the life young men are to be consigned to when they enter upon a military career? However disgraceful and humiliating as the Windsor courts-martial have been, the newsaper stressed that it did not believe that all regiments are as tainted as the 46th. Most commanding officers are men of unstained honour and blameless life, models which younger officers would do well to imitate. The scandals of the 46th would never have occurred under their auspices. One great principle of life in the army is that a regiment takes its tone from the commanding officer. Colonel Garrett must be judged by this simple and universal rule. Lord Hardinge may or may not adopt a sterner method in dealing with this officer and the mess room of the 46th, but at least he must put an end to the protracted scandal of these courts-martial upon an inoffensive and outraged young subaltern.

The following day there were more letters in the newspaper: forwarding subscriptions to the Perry defence fund; and suggesting that the 'officers and gentlemen' [the correspondent's italics] who were it seems determined to 'smash Perry' should be given the earliest opportunity to go and smash the enemy, and should be sent forward in advance of the allied forces, armed with empty champagne bottles or pieces of broken door, etc. to smash the Tsar himself and end the war. Others testified to the high character of Perry when a school-fellow of a correspondent's son; and finally explaining that the delay was not of Lord Hardinge's making. The last letter set out the invariable practice. When the court-martial has finished its deliberations the proceedings are sealed up and sent to the Judge Advocate's office. They are considered by him and are then passed to Her Majesty with his legal opinion. When the Queen has considered them they are transmitted to the Commander-in-Chief and only then is Lord Hardinge officially cognisant of the proceedings. It is then his duty to go into the case and submit to Her Majesty his observations, having regard to questions of a military nature, with reference to giving effect to the finding and sentence of the court.

For a few days nothing was heard of the case but on Monday the 4th of September *The Times* wrote that the verdict on Perry must be close, for the Deputy Judge Advocate had been seen by the Queen and the case must have been discussed. In the newspaper's opinion, it would not have been difficult to adduce fifty reasons why the proceedings of the court should be quashed and set aside, if the same rules of evidence apply to the decision on the honour of an English officer as obtain in the case of an urchin who is charged with the most trumpery theft. Court martial law may be different but the ultimate decision in the case rests with Lord Hardinge, the Commander-in-Chief. He bears a heavy responsibility but it may guide him in his decision if he accepts that at well-nigh every dinner-table and in every private dwelling it is believed that a spirit of profligacy and debauchment exists among the officers in too many of the regiments in the Queen's service. In various barracks drunkeness prevails, young women are debauched, and common strumpets are brought in before the face of the soldiers who might be put under arrest for the slightest disrespect to those officers involved. It is believed that oppression and exclusion is organized in many regiments against any young officer who will not join in these shameful follies, and night after night scenes of riot and violence prevail, as we have heard in the revelations from the 46th Regiment. As far as the bulk of the officers is concerned, that regiment is disgraceful and discreditable to the Queen's service. There should have been an inquiry into the conduct of the officers of that regiment and mainly into that of the commanding officer. Lord Hardinge should look elsewhere than to the phalanx of officers giving evidence whose sole virtue is fidelity to each other. He should consult the people of Belfast, or Chester, where the regiment had been stationed. They could throw light on the conduct of Colonel Garrett and his young friends. If Lord Hardinge, had put the affair in the hands of a detective officer he would in a few hours have received some very edifying information as to the conduct of those involved. It is all very sad and disgraceful and the only cheering point in the whole case was the public outrage at the abused form of military justice applied to Perry. The subscription organised by the Mayor of Windsor to bear his legal costs was evidence of this but no amount could compensate him for the mental torture he must have undergone. Englishmen will not tolerate the oppression of individuals under a form of law which applied in the more evil times of our history. Such a case of military oppression might have occurred in any European country but in none would public opinion have come to the rescue with such instant and decisive force. However at present the decision was with Lord Hardinge, but it should not be delayed.

The verdict on Greer

The same day there were two important developments. First, the sentence on Lieutenant Greer was announced. He had been tried, of course, charged with conduct unbecoming an officer and gentleman to the prejudice of good order and military discipline for:

1. Having wilfully struck and offered other personal violence to Perry, and

2. Having at the same time used provoking, insulting and disgusting language to Perry, calling him 'swindler', 'blackguard', and using other language of an offensive and insulting nature.

Readers who have noted the overwhelming evidence against him will be surprised that he was acquitted of the charges. Nevertheless he was ordered to 'sell out', a strange punishment if he was not guilty of the charges against him.

The Commander-in-Chief also punished Lieutenant William Thomas Waldy though he had never been subject of any formal charges. He was ordered to be severely reprimanded, in consequence of his conduct in connection with the letter written by him to Lieutenant Perry and produced in court after his denying its contents.

But the other main accused had been Perry, and he was not so lucky as Greer.

Perry

Having survived the first trial which had effectively been quashed for irregularities, *The Times* reported on 5th September that Perry had been on that same Monday, 4th September, summoned to the Officers' Mess Room at the Windsor Sheet Street barracks and with Major Maxwell and Adjutant M'Alister present, Lieutenant Colonel Garrett had read to him the sentence of the Horse Guards. He was acquitted of the first charge against him. This was that in his letter to Colonel Upton, president of Greer's court martial, he had slandered his commanding officer, Lieutenant Colonel Garrett, by stating that when he had reported repeated acts of violence to him from brother officers the colonel had reproached him and called him a fool for his pains. The full enormity of this acquittal - meaning that the court had not believed Garrett's own evidence - appears to have escaped the authorities at Horse Guards.

The remaining three charges were that in the same letter Perry had written that he had threatened Garrett that he would appeal to the General, knowing that was false; that in the trial of Greer he had testified that Nicholas had ill-treated young officers on joining, knowing that to be false; and that in that same trial he had written to the officiating Deputy Judge Advocate with the same allegation about Nicholas knowing it to be false. On all three he was found guilty. The court recommended mercy on the grounds of his youth and inexperience, and as he had acted on the advice of his legal adviser.

In the light of that recommendation, and also on the ground of the long and meritorious services of his father, the Commander-in-Chief, under the sanction of Her Majesty, dismissed Perry from the Service but allowed him to sell his commission.

Indignation and fury from Press and public

In the same issue that reported the verdicts and sentences, *The Times* printed an incandescent 'leader' commenting on the verdict on Perry. 'This most scandalous verdict has received the sanction of the Commander-in-Chief. Since the days of the infamous Jeffreys in England there has been nothing like this trial. Revolutionary France might show plenty of analogous cases but no one could rely on such precedents. The mischief done by the verdict can never be undone. A Court of fifteen officers has brought in a monstrous verdict and the C-in-C has sanctioned it. In no other court could such a verdict have been obtained on such testimony. Though it was odious and disgusting to do so, the newspaper reviewed the leading points of the case. Perry had been effectively charged on three points. The fact that on the first, falsely claiming that Colonel Garrett had dismissed his complaint and called him a 'fool for his pains', he had been found not guilty meant that Garrett was guilty not only of such conduct, but also of swearing on oath that he did not use the epithet in question. This was the commanding officer of Her Majesty's 46th Regiment. If the subaltern is to be dismissed, what does this commanding officer deserve?

The second point related to Perry's assertion that he had sent his colonel a letter of complaint addressed to the general of the district. Garrett denied this and could recollect nothing of the sort. He produced other officers to say that they remembered nothing of it. But there was a violent probability that such an affair might have taken place from the ruffianly tone of this regiment - and there was specific evidence to confirm this before the court. Captain and Paymaster Corcoran gave clear evidence of young officers complaining to him about 'practical jokes' which amounted to harsh and improper conduct towards them, including Perry. Perry had come to him the day after writing the letter concerned and had said that several officers were urging him to withdraw it. Could Perry, under the influence of second sight, have staged this scene with Corcoran over a year before to help his case? Would any other twelve English gentlemen have reached such a verdict?

The third point, the subject of the third and fourth charges, concerned Captain Nicholas. Perry had asserted that he was a bully towards young officers. A procession of officers was produced who all duly swore that they remembered nothing of such behaviour. But one of them had actually written to Perry describing a specific incident of Nicholas - this chivalric and spotless officer, a model of deportment and courtesy - had behaved abominably to a young officer at the regiment's mess table, in front of several officers. How could Lord Hardinge confirm this discreditable verdict?

162

The matter must not be allowed to rest. The profession of arms would be disgraced. The truth is that, as evidenced by this regiment, the moral condition of the officers in the army is at the lowest possible ebb. And there is not just vulgar riot and profligacy. The court-martial proceedings constitute a far more appalling revelation than the extravagant blackguards of a single regiment. Perry has been unjustly condemned but it is the highest administration of the army that is called in question. How can the Queen expect gentlemen to wear her uniform when their honour and position in society can be imperilled before such a tribunal as has now brought disgrace upon the British army. The principle of justice may have been for the moment trampled underfoot but it cannot be quenched. We commit the case of Lieutenant Perry into the hands of his countrymen.

Nor was *The Times* alone in its condemnation. Perhaps surprisingly, *Colburn's United Services Magazine,* a monthly journal widely read by service officers, and of course by many retired officers and gentlemen, was equally forthright about the court-martial procedures and the state of the 46th Foot. Its issue for September 1854 wrote that the recent Courts-Martial at Windsor possess an importance which it would be impossible to over-rate, and will assuredly exercise, in their effect, a very considerable influence on the future welfare of the Army. No judicial proceeding for many years has exerted the same interest in the country, and it is now understood, for the first time, how the hydra of authority, when it has a purpose to answer, can bear down with crushing weight on the helpless and innocent. It is in the interest of every officer and every man in both the services that such a state of things should cease, and the irresistible voice of the press has announced to those in power that tyranny and oppression, however disguised, will no longer be tolerated, let them be attempted by whom they may. This, the voice of the press, and not the Court of Officers at Windsor, is the great tribunal at which Lieutenant Perry has been arraigned, tried and unhesitatingly acquitted! It needed not his touching and eloquent defence, in which he pointed out the utter worthlessness of the evidence, as well as the partiality of the prosecutor, to establish beyond doubt a universal conviction of his innocence. The naked rottenness of the case was already patent to every eye. The day has come when, even in the Army and Navy, tyranny must pursue its devices in secret, if it wishes to escape exposure. A detailed analysis of the evidence followed and the magazine closed with the comment that the result of the trial would shortly be known but whatever the result there can be but one opinion as to the character of the witnesses for the prosecution.

In a separate 'leader' *Colburn's* also commented on 'the state of the 46th Regiment'. It suggested that the disgraceful condition of the regiment, as exhibited in the recent revelations, calls imperatively for still further inquiry. The men can not feel any respect for their officers, who have been ridiculed in *Punch,* lampooned in the public streets, and made the subject of derisive songs and ballads. The disclosures made at the courts-martial have cast a stigma on the character of the whole British Army. The proud appellation of 'officer and gentleman', which the service has so long, so jealously, and so honourably preserved, is now brought in question. Throughout the service it is the wish that this stigma should be instantly wiped off. Lord Hardinge has but one course to pursue; and what it is, they wrote, we need not point out. They were to be disappointed.

On September 6th, *The Times* printed the full text of the general orders issued from Horse Guards on August 9th and later dates, by command of the General Commanding- in-Chief, above the signature of the Military Secretary, Major General Charles

Yorke, on the subject of the courts-martial and they are significant in revealing the thinking behind the punishments inflicted.

On 9th August they first set out the charge at Perry's first court-martial - his assault on Greer. The court's decision was as follows:

'The court having maturely weighed and considered the evidence in support of the prosecution, together with what the prisoner, Lieutenant James Edward Perry, 46th Regiment, has urged in his defence, does now find, and is of opinion, that he is guilty of the charges preferred against him, which being in breach of the Articles of War, does now sentence the prisoner to be dismissed Her Majesty's service' but also quoted the letter to the Judge-Advocate-General, dated 14th July, from the President, Brevet Colonel James Lindsay, Grenadier Guards: 'Sir, I am requested by the unanimous desire of the members of the court-martial of which I am President to recommend the prisoner to the favourable consideration of Her Majesty, in consequences of his youth and the amount of gross provocation he appears to have received from Lieutenant Greer of his regiment.'

There followed a legal ruling: It appeared that the Court had been cleared to decide if Perry could be allowed to put this question to Greer during the latter's cross-examination:
'Did you not seize me by the breast and throat, and throw me on the bed, and did I not order you under arrest, which you refused to obey, saying you would see me d-------d first?'
The Court had not allowed this question to be put and, acting in the absence of the Judge-Advocate-General, the Deputy Judge-Advocate-General was of opinion that the question was legally admissible and relevant to the issue. It should have been allowed and he therefore submitted to Her Majesty that she should

not confirm the proceedings. Therefore, as communicated earlier, the proceedings were not confirmed.

On September 2nd, General Order 542 (*reproduced in full at Appendix E*), stated the position on Greer's Court-Martial. The charge was in two parts. The first alleged that he had wilfully struck and offered personal violence to Perry, and the second that he had used provoking, insulting and disgusting language to him, by calling him 'swindler', 'blackguard', and other expressions of a most offensive and insulting nature.

The Court had found Greer not guilty of the first part - having struck Perry - but found him guilty of the second part except for use of the words 'swindler' and 'blackguard'. They sentenced him to be severely reprimanded, and to be reduced on the list of lieutenants in his regiment, being placed next below Lieutenant Dunscombe.

The Deputy Judge-Advocate-General noted that two particular witnesses had given evidence, Perry himself, and the woman Esther Major. Perry had given positive and detailed evidence of several distinct acts of personal violence committed against him by Greer and there was no ground for deeming his evidence less worthy of credit by his cross-examination. Esther Major's evidence did not directly confirm particular details of the personal violence but did not contradict it and seemed to corroborate it by agreeing in many particulars. There seemed no doubt that acts of personal violence were committed by Greer and that he used the expressions specified in the second part of the charge. Neither the evidence adduced by Greer, nor his address, could impair or alter the effect of the evidence against him. It thus appeared that the Court's finding on the first part was without warrant as being against evidence, and that part of their finding on the second part which related to the words 'swindler' and 'blackguard' was also without warrant as being against evidence. Her Majesty was advised to order the Court to re-assemble with a view to revising their proceedings and duly did so.

On 11th August 1854 the Court re-assembled as instructed. Having carefully re-considered the evidence that was brought before them during the trial, they begged most respectfully to adhere to their former decision. The Queen did not confirm or approve the finding and sentence of the Court, and the General Commanding-in-Chief submitted to her Majesty his view of Greer's conduct throughout the matter. As a witness in Perry's first trial he had repeatedly refused to answer the questions put to him by Perry, on the plea that he would thereby incriminate himself, though answers were necessary for the discovery of the truth. In his own trial it was clearly established by evidence that he had applied the most disgusting expressions to Perry. Evidence in Perry's first trial confirmed those facts and they admitted of no reasonable doubt. Such ungentlemanly conduct is calculated to degrade an officer in the eyes of his men, and to destroy his power of maintaining discipline. A person who does not shrink from the utterance of such disgraceful language is unfit to preserve his position of social equality in a regiment among his brother officers. Nor could he exchange into another regiment as the officers would refuse to receive him, and they would be entitled so to do under Her Majesty's regulations.

The General Commanding-in-Chief could not omit to mark his severest displeasure of the gambling propensities of Greer, but even without those propensities the misconduct already noted is sufficient to call for his removal from the army. Her Majesty was therefore advised that Greer should be removed from the service by the sale of his commission and to this she agreed.

General Order 543 of 2nd September 1854 *(reproduced in full at Appendix F)* dealt with Perry's second trial. Despite the recommendation of the Court in his favour, the C-in-C felt that the importance of upholding discipline and good order necessitated that the sentence passed by the Court should be carried into effect. No commanding officer would be safe in the discharge of his duties if inferior officers could with impunity make accusations similar to those of which Perry had been found guilty. He had been acquitted on the first charge, but found guilty on the second, third and fourth charges. He had been sentenced to be cashiered. When an officer has been found guilty of such charges, and sentenced to be cashiered, and when the legality of the proceedings has been confirmed by the two departments whose duty it is to advise Her Majesty, there is only one way of giving effect to the Court's recommendation for clemency. That is for the C-in-C to solicit the Queen to allow the prisoner to receive the value of his commission, and this Her Majesty had graciously approved. Perry had been appointed to an ensigncy in January 1853, without purchase, solely on account of his father's very meritorious services in the army, and he had subsequently purchased his lieutenancy.

The C-in-C went on to state that he could not fail to comment on Lieutenant William Waldy's letter dated 2nd June 1854 and addressed to Perry[155]. It could not be reconciled with

---

[155] A Court of Enquiry had been set up under Major General Yorke, Military Secretary, to enquire if Waldy's behaviour was sufficient to bring charges with a reasonable prospect of obtaining a conviction by a General Court Martial. The Deputy Judge Advocate General advised there was not, and suggested that Waldy should apologise to Ensign Coote and Captain Nicholas, and that Viscount Hardinge, the General Commanding-in-Chief, might wish to reprimand him. As noted at the end of the

Waldy's evidence given at the court-martial a few weeks afterwards. In the letter he had stated that Captain Nicholas had applied a very insulting epithet to Ensign Coote at the mess-table and Coote had given the lie direct to Nicholas. As a witness on oath before the court-martial he denied, or claimed to forget, that he had written such a letter.

Even if he had forgotten, his levity deserves the severest reprehension. After the court had closed, Waldy had been called upon by his commanding officer to explain his conduct. Waldy had said: 'he must have given a higher colour to the affair than it merited', that 'since the affair scarce an officer had spoken to him' and that 'in a foolish moment he wrote the strong language recorded against him in his letter'. Waldy appeared to be a weak, gossiping young man, insensible of the duty of a rigid adherence to the truth in describing the conduct of others, and incapable of estimating the mischievous consequences of exaggerating a contradiction at the mess-table into the lie direct, by which departure from the truth of the character of his brother officers might have been seriously affected. As, however, he did not appear to have been actuated by malice, and in the absence of any proof of corrupt intention, the General Commanding- in-Chief hereby directs, with the sanction of Her Majesty, that Lieutenant William Waldy be severely reprimanded and cautioned for the rest of his life to adhere strictly to the truth.

The same day, September 2nd, the C-in-C issued a memorandum signed by the Deputy Adjutant General, Major General George Augustus Wetherall, 'apropos of the late

---

paragraph, he duly did so. See WO 81/99. At age 81 Waldy wrote his memoirs and says nothing of the Windsor days, but does record that ragging and drinking - sometimes all night - were very prevalent. Waldy, *From Eight to Eighty,* pub 1914.

revelations of the manners and customs of the 46th'. In brief it read as follows[156].

It regretted that in the last year it had twice been necessary to remind every regiment that a few inconsiderate officers could bring their regiment into disrepute unless in their social conduct towards each other their behaviour should be regulated by a higher standard of what is expected of their honourable position as holders of commissions in Her Majesty's army. The first case had occurred in the 50th Regiment where four subalterns were court-martialled for forcibly seizing a young ensign, taking him to a pump, and there pumping on him. Two officers were dismissed and two were reprimanded. Lord Hardinge had issued a memorandum on 5th July 1853[157] which had been read to the officers of every regiment in the service.

Despite this, in the 62nd Regiment in October 1853, a captain in command of two companies had repeatedly annoyed and disturbed the subaltern of his own company, and accompanied by other officers, had been in the habit of bursting into his room, and taking his bed to pieces. The lieutenant had reported this to the major of his regiment and the commanding officer had reported the case to the Horse Guards. The captain was removed to another regiment and lost five steps towards his advancement. One subaltern was also removed, but a second captain was retained in the 62nd at the intercession of his commanding officer on account of his good service in the field in India, from which the regiment had but lately returned. Again, the facts were circulated and read to the officers of every regiment.

---

[156] The full text is at Appendix B.
[157] Summarised in Wetherall's Memo at Appendix B.

Now a third case had occurred, this time in the 46th Regiment. There had been disgraceful deep gambling in a barrack room at Windsor by Lieutenants Greer and Perry terminating in a violent assault, and the use by Greer of disgusting language to Perry. At the end of Greer's court-martial, Perry had handed in a letter charging his commanding officer, Colonel Garrett, with grave acts of injustice and stating that Perry had written to him threatening to appeal to the general officer of the district. Colonel Garrett denied the acts, and that any such letter had ever been sent to him.

The General Commanding-in-Chief was determined not to allow any compromise, but to eradicate the unmanly system. Perry's charges had been specific and amounted to a breach of Her Majesty's regulations. They were also in defiance of the admonitions and orders circulated in July and December 1853. It was resolved, therefore, that the truth or falsehood of these charges should be investigated by a court-martial on oath. The result of that court-martial had now been circulated and every young officer may thus have, on joining his regiment, a clear understanding of his own position. He must carefully read the Articles of War and the letter of the Judge Advocate published with those articles in 1844[158], together with the Articles[159] and the Mutiny Act.

If the ensign is firm, and has the proper spirit of an officer and a gentleman, he can without any loss of honour or of temper, resist coarse practical jokes. If he submits to them on the plea that

---

[158] The Judge Advocate's letter of 20 March 1844 and the observations of the Secretary at War are reproduced in full at Appendix C1.
[159] The relevant Articles of War are reproduced in full at Appendix C2.

they are the customary probation of an officer entering the British army he will justly have tamely submitted to insult, and it is his duty that he should not suffer any liberties to be taken which would expose him to the derision of his brother officers and the men under his command.

It is said that coarse irregularities, termed practical jokes, and the use of disgusting language have increased since the 1844 Articles, as they more strictly prohibited duelling in the army, following a duel the previous year between two officers who were brothers-in-law in which one was killed. But the real reason for the stricter articles prohibiting duelling was that the tone of society had improved and all men were united in abhorring so barbarous a mode of settling a dispute. Since the change a few men of coarse and ungenerous tempers may have taken greater liberties with their brother officers but such practices cannot be permitted. They must be repressed for they are degrading to the character of an officer and render him unfit to command his men who cannot feel for him the respect which is the basis of all enduring authority. They also render him unfit to associate with his brother officers who must hold him in contempt. The manners of British officers must never fall below the standard recognized by gentlemen and behaviour which would formerly have led to a duel must now lead to the removal of the offender from the society of which he has shown himself to be an unworthy member.

Every assistance and support must be given to young officers in their endeavours to avoid such consequences. The captain of the company a young officer joins is to give him advice and support and the regiment's major is to do the same and will be held responsible for doing it effectually. If any case arises requiring interference or reprimand the details must be reported to the general and sent up to Horse Guards. All serious cases will be reported to the Adjutant-General for decision by the General Commanding-in-Chief.

The notes from Horse Guards ended with this: General Viscount Hardinge cofidently asserts that the regimental system of the British army, now so long established, has proved its efficiency as being admirably adapted for all the duties of war and peace. He trusts that the irregularities and mischievous tendencies resulting from practical jokes can and will be corrected and disappear for ever. A firm but temperate exercise of authority on the part of commanding officers will achieve this, and they will find by a faithful discharge of their duty that they will obtain the respect and support of their officer and the esteem of their fellow-subjects.

The next day, September 7th, *The Times* returned to the subject in a leader beginning: If there were any consonance between the professions and the practice of the Horse Guards, Mr Perry would at this moment have been acquitted, Mr Greer have been summarily dismissed from the Queen's service, Lieutenant Waldy be lying under an indictment for perjury, and Colonel Garrett be brought before a suitable tribunal to answer for his conduct since he has been in command of the 46th Regiment. They had earlier, of course, been biting in their criticism of Garrett and now approved of the spirit of Lord Hardinge's orders but lamented that he was the first person to set them at defiance. He should be told, and his Royal Mistress should understand, that the outrage perpetrated on this young officer against all justice and common sense would lower in the public mind the character of every officer who holds the Queen's commission. The way in which the second trial was conducted was scandalous, and its finding was in barefaced defiance of the evidence. As a way to test the evidence against Colonel Garrett, it gave him every advantage and laid his accuser under every difficulty, indeed it was only by an oppressive stretch of power that a second charge against Mr Perry was fudged up at all. He was the subject of a scandalous outrage. Every officer in his regiment was turned against him in his first trial and after escaping by a miracle he was sent to trial again upon charges which could only be made good by testimony from those who were bitterly hostile to him and only needed to 'forget' in order to secure his expulsion from the service. Nevertheless, despite being unable to cross-examine these miserable creatures who were brought in, one after the other, to say they had 'really forgotten', he made out a defence which should have made it impossible for the fifteen officers of the court to believe that he had maliciously and wilfully lied when he asserted that Garrett had called him a fool, that he had threatened to complain to the general, and that a man named Nicholas was a bully.

Hardinge sanctioned the finding and has now issued a set of General Orders of the purest morality and high-toned chivalry. What a pity that Hardinge ignored them to turn Perry out of the army for following them. Parents should examine the happenings at Windsor carefully and draw from them a serious conclusion. Why trust the future of a beloved to such? The series of Court-Martials shows that blackguardism is not only in one regiment. Some forty officers, including a large proportion of Lieutenant-Colonels commanding regiments, have taken part, have found young Perry guilty and dismissed him from the service, acquitted Greer, and verbally reprimanded the lad whose evidence was perjury. To these men a lad's future would be committed if a parent was so ill-advised as to purchase a commission in the Queen's service. Dangers in battle or sickness on campaign are as nothing compared with the perils of army life as an officer. The bottle and the brothel are the order of the day and woe to him if he tries to avoid the customs of the army. Young Perry tried it and note the result. He will be avoided, affronted, assaulted, subjected to personal indignity, and when finally exasperated into resistance the chapter of courts-martial will commence. The truth or falsehood of accusations which may be trumped up against him have nothing to do with the result. If by a miracle an acquittal should be obtained, another charge, another and another, will be got up until the desired effect is produced. Nor will any protection come from the Commander-in-Chief. The moral tone of the British army is at present most deplorably low, not merely as regards debauchery but in the principles of common honesty and truth. The prestige of the British officer is at an end, the Queen's uniform obtains no respect.

How shall the honour of the British officer be restored? First, the system of courts-martial must be ended. The form of proceedings is so antiquated and ridiculous that justice is well-nigh unattainable. The mess system, so long considered an advantage, fails when the facts are considered. The ruffianism and brutality are not confined to the 46th Regiment, but prevail widely throughout the British service even though scandals have previously been hushed up by secret courts of inquiry. Colonels scratch each other's backs and the Commander-in-Chief approves. The matter cannot be suffered to remain in its present condition. As for Mr Perry, we cannot but congratulate him on having escaped from such disreputable associates.

Predictably the next day, Friday 8th September, brought letters highly critical of the way that Perry had been treated. 'T.O.B.' thought that Hardinge must have been under some form of hallucination to ratify the extraordinary sentence. Had he assumed that if Perry was acquitted the reputation of the whole army would be compromised, and so sacrificed an innocent person? Some means must be found to purge the military profession. There had recently been a Royal Commission on sewers which had reported on many kinds of filth. Let there now be one on the causes of the pernicious atmosphere in some officers' quarters. Then let regulations be issued for the immediate purification of such quarters from all unwholesome influences, unclean bodies, refuse characters and the like. Let all offenders against such regulations be tried. Surely if we can abate the cholera we can prevent barrack rooms from becoming the source of moral infection. As for justice to offenders, we have no difficulty in civil courts so why should we accept blundering by military courts. Apart from the injustice to Mr Perry, take the incomprehensible award in Greer's case. He was 'Acquitted but ordered to sell out.' In the name of common sense how can a prisoner be acquitted and still be punished? This military judge and jury will ever be remembered for such nonsense.

Another writer lamented the circumstances and suggested that those who agreed with him should now show their feelings by subscribing to a fund for Mr Perry to make him independent of his enemies, the ruffians of the 46th Regiment.

The next day one writing as 'Cedant arma togae' ('let arms yield to gown', i.e. 'military authority yield to the civil power') suggested three actions to Perry and his advisers. First, a civil action in trespass against those who have destroyed his property and assaulted him. Second, an indictment of perjury against at least one of his accusers, and Thirdly an indictment for conspiracy against his colonel and most of the witnesses.

Instead, perhaps doubting the practicality of such potential remedies, Perry's friends, who had already opened a Defence Fund, decided to petition the Queen praying that she should order the entire proceedings of the three courts-martial to be reviewed by civil judges, and that she should then give a final decision. Meanwhile the fund proceeded most satisfactorily with the Mayor of Windsor, who acted as Treasurer, receiving letters and subscriptions by every post.

To widespread surprise, the two lieutenant vacancies in the 46th were not filled as normally they would have been, by the two senior ensigns but instead Lieutenant Thomas John Barlow Connell, with seniority (by purchase) 24 March 1854, transferred from the 3rd West Indies Regiment of Foot, and Lieutenant the Hon. William Henry Herbert, with seniority, also by purchase, 25 August 1854 transferred from the 43rd Monmouth Foot (Light Infantry). Thus no ensign received an automatic 'step' to fill the vacancies as they would have done if the two seniors had purchased the vacancies and two new ensigns had been placed at the bottom of the list. This was, in a sense, a collective punishment and a sign of Horse Guards disapproval of the 46th.

Public reaction

Meanwhile there was evidence of public disapproval too in the town of Windsor of the officers of the 46th. They were saluted with *'non mi recordo'*, or 'I don't recollect' as they passed by and women congregated at the corners of the streets and lanes and abused them. Two ballad hawkers arrived from London with a plentiful supply of papers entitled 'The Court-Martial at Windsor' and did a brisk trade. However when they approached the Town Hall they were set upon by a party of soldiers and had to be rescued, and sent packing, by the police. There were other incidents in the town and the newspaper feared for serious disturbances if the 46th were not removed. An incident on the river Thames was reported. A party of tradesmen from Eton boating near Swansbridge came upon a boat of officers and shouted insults. The officers ran their boat alongside the tradesmen and a splashing match ensued until one tradesman found a large scoop in his boat and drenched the officers forcing their rapid repeat. And walking in Windsor High-street, Major Maxwell and Adjutant M'Alister were taunted by two youths calling 'Don't you remember?' and 'I have no recollection, whatsoever.' Remarkably, Maxwell ordered a passing soldier to take one of the youths, named Simms, into custody and convey him to the police station. Simms was brought before the magistrates, charged with insulting Maxwell and M'Alister. Maxwell swore to the circumstances noted above, but said that he didn't want the youth punished but as he and his brother officers had been so frequently insulted in this way wished to show that such insults could not be offered with impunity. He hoped the magistrates would give the lad advice and admonition which he could communicate to other lads. Mr Voules, defending Simms, declared that he needed to offer no defence as the offence charged was no offence in law and the Mayor, presiding, agreed. That was perfectly clear, but nevertheless he hoped that no further annoyance would be offered to the officers and soldiers in garrison.

Further correspondence in the newspapers led to the Duke of Cleveland criticising Colonel Garrett for the disgraceful condition of the regiment's internal discipline and Garrett demanded to know what evidence there was of this. Predictably, an anonymous writer to *The Times* ('A Civilian') answered him in forthright terms. 'We have heard from the lips of witnesses whose veracity was not shaken, that his officers have for years been in the habit of smashing in each other's doors, of ducking each other in the water, of stripping each other naked in public, &c; and bearing in mind the mode in which his young friends gave, or rather did not give, their evidence on Lieutenant Perry's courts-martial, cannot but unanimously coincide with the Duke in the view he has taken of both colonel and officers of the 46th Regiment. There is not a single man of sense and honour in the

United Kingdom who would see, without dismay, his son appointed to a regiment under the command of Colonel Garrett; nor is there a city or town which would not learn with disgust that the corps which that gallant officer commands was about to be quartered in its precincts.'

Epilogue

The conclusion of the trials was followed promptly by the move to the Crimea of the main body of the regiment - two companies and a party under Lieutenant Dallas had, of course, gone ahead in August 1854 before the completion of the trial. Dallas's party, on the transport *Harbinger,* was apparently a Guard of Honour for General Cathcart who was to command the 4th Division, or perhaps to guard the substantial quantity of gold being shipped to the East. The two companies were commanded by Captain Hardy and included Lieutenants Shervinton, Knapp, O'Toole, Helyar and Townsend. Perry had complained - to no avail - that the officers sent in that way, ahead of the main body, had been chosen to remove witnesses that he might have wished to give evidence in his defence.

In the event, as part of the 4th Division, the two companies and Dallas's group landed at Old Fort on 20/21 September 1854 but were left there, attached to the 63rd Regiment, as Rear Party and arrived at the scene of the Battle of Alma late in the day, after the conflict was over. They then fought bravely at Inkerman on 5th November, again with the 63rd as part of 4th Division, being involved with General Cathcart's ill-fated attempt to counter-attack which resulted in the general's death, allegedly exclaiming, as he fell, 'Well done, the 46th!'[160]

---

[160] The other regiment involved in this incident, the 68th, believe that Cathcart's words were: 'Well done, the 68th!'

The main body arrived in Balaklava Harbour on 7th November and disembarked the next day.[161] That afternoon, in a fine state of health except for five men left at the General Hospital, marched up to the heights of Sevastopol where they joined the two companies which had gone ahead. The total strength, including the two companies was about 900. Their tents, however, did not arrive until 4 o'clock the next morning and thus the troops were exposed to the rain and cold night air on their first night after landing. On the very next day, 9th November, upwards of 500 men were detailed for duty in the trenches and on the 10th cholera broke out amongst them. On the 14th, the tents were overturned in the violent hurricane which struck the area and during the remainder of the month it rained almost continuously, while the men had no other protection from the damp ground than a mat or a single blanket. At first the tour of duty in the trenches lasted 24 hours, but on the 16th, owing to the severity of the weather, the men in the trenches were relieved every 12 hours. But for eight or nine consecutive days every disposable man in the regiment was marched to the trenches at 4.30 p.m., returning at 6.30 a.m. the next day. They were without warm clothing, on a short allowance of rations, and in want of fuel. Health rapidly deteriorated. Diarrhoea became almost universal and 268 cases of cholera occurred between the 10th and 30th of the month. 56 per cent of the strength was admitted to hospital and 86 died - only three from wounds inflicted by the enemy. During December duties continued to be extremely severe, with the men almost continuously in the trenches, on fatigue duties to Balaklava, or on camp guards. Rations were often issued too late to be properly cooked and anyway there was little fuel available to cook. Over

---

[161] These notes are taken from the Official Medical History, printed by order in Parliamentary Papers, 1857-8 Vol XXXVIII. See also 'The Murder of a Regiment', pub 1994, ISBN 1-899244-00-X, ed by the present author.

69 per cent of strength were admitted into the Regimental Hospital and 66 died, over half from illness other than cholera. January 1855 was no better. Over 100 per cent of strength were under medical treatment at some time during the month and 61 died. As the winter passed, conditions improved slowly but through the whole time in Crimea 2,840 cases were admitted into hospital from that original strength of 900.

Operationally, the regiment was camped on elevated ground to the extreme left of the 4th Division and about 600 yards from Cathcart's Hill. They remained there during the whole period of military operations before Sevastopol. For the assault on the Redan on 18th June 1855 they formed part of the Right Attack, Force Reserve but were not committed and suffered no casualties. In the final assault on 8th September they were again Force Reserve, this time for the Left Attack, were not committed, and suffered just one man killed.

In May 1856 the regiment left Crimea for Corfu and stayed there until moving to India in 1858.

And the men...

And what became of the individuals involved in the trial?

James Perry, sentenced to be dismissed, but allowed to sell his commission, was now famous, and Madame Tussaud's Waxworks proudly announced that a wax figure of him had been added to their display. His defence fund, the *Perry Defence and Testimonial Fund,* administered by the Mayor of Windsor, had received over two thousand pounds in public subscriptions. After legal expenses and advertising, the balance was invested in the joint names of Perry and the mayor. It was to have been expended in the purchase of his promotion in the army if the verdict of the court-martial had been set aside, as was confidently expected but not realised. Otherwise the fund was to be placed at Perry's disposal to promote his best interests as a civilian. Some embarrassment was experienced by the Administrator when Mr Perry went to Paris and on 4th November 1854 attempted, unsuccessfully, to have one thousand five hundred pounds transferred from the London and County Joint Stock Bank, where the money was lodged, to his credit at the Charles du Buits in Paris. The fund was then closed and the treasurer placed a notice in the newspapers asking that no more subscriptions be sent in. The money remained deposited with the Windsor bankers. In August 1855 Perry with his father Charles James Perry, Paymaster of the 87th Regiment (Irish Fusiliers), who had come over from India expressly for the purpose, went to Windsor 'for the purpose of settling this long-winded affair.' His father had been commissioned from the ranks as Quartermaster on 23 July 1844, promoted to Ensign on 22 December 1848 and to Lieutenant on 30 November 1849. He was appointed Paymaster on 3 May 1850. (He was placed on half pay on 16 August 1859 having been in India throughout the war.)

While in England Perry Senior sought a commission for his son in the Turkish Legion but was unsuccessful. The son went to Australia and there in Melbourne finally collected the balance of his fund, some two thousand and ten pounds. A total of £2632 had been collected[162], expenses had been £472 and £149 had already been paid to Perry. Thorough research in Australia has found no references to him, and he probably returned to England. There is

---

[162] An idea of the various subscribers, from the Duke of Marlborough who sent £50, to one shilling from 'A poor tradesman', is shown in the advertisement from *The Times* for 2nd September 1854.

an intriguing notice in *The Times* of 30 December 1875 which asks 'Perry, late of the 46th Regt but now believed to be a wine merchant' to get in touch with a Plymouth solicitor. This may well have been our man. No more is heard of him until on 3 March 1886, some thirty-two years after his disgrace, his father, Charles James Perry, then living in Teddington in Middlesex, died and Letters of Administration were granted to James Perry, described in the grant as 'Lieutenant in Her Majesty's Army (retired)' which was no doubt how he had styled himself – inaccurately - after being cashiered. Even more surprising is to find him in the High Court of Justice, Probate Division, thirteen years later, in the case of Perry v. Rixon[163]. Miss Ada Rixon, a spinster, had died on 18 November 1898 and in her will executed in 1891 had left all her estate amounting to four thousand pounds to James Edward Perry, described by counsel for her trustee as 'a total stranger'. She had even expressed the wish that her funeral be the simplest and least expensive possible to maximise the residue available. The clue to this mystery is in her wish to be buried at Brookwood Cemetery, Woking, 'beside Charles James Perry' and in brackets appear the explanatory words '(Colonel Perry's father)' [sic]. The suggestion that James had now become a colonel is extraordinary, and we can only deduce that his father, Charles Perry, had become close to Miss Rixon, so that five years after his death, when she executed her will, she wished to leave all her estate to the son, a total stranger, and that either she was confused about army ranks and entitlement to them, or James had promoted himself from Lieutenant (which he was not) to Colonel (which he certainly was not.) No record has yet been found of his death.

Greer left the regiment in 1854, allowed to 'sell out', receiving the value of his commission and disappears from sight.

---

[163] Reported in *The Times* for 21 March 1899.

Major Maxwell succeeded to command of the regiment in December 1854 when he was promoted Lieutenant Colonel. Major Vesey then became the regimental Major, and Lieutenant Colonel in August 1858. Captain Campbell was promoted Brevet Lieutenant Colonel in November 1855 after serving as an Assistant Engineer and being wounded in the trenches. All three received awards of the Turkish Order of the Medjidie and the first two received French awards as well. Captains Nicholas and M'Alester received Turkish awards. Major Fyffe returned home for medical reasons in January 1855.

Captain O'Toole who had taken the first two companies to the East died of disease on 21 September 1854. He was succeeded by Captain William Hardy who was himself wounded at Inkerman and invalided home in November 1854. Captain Fred Dallas brought the companies out of the battle of Inkerman and was later promoted Brevet Major. Captain Shervinton, Lieutenants Knapp, Helyer (wounded), and Townshend were all in the advance party and fought at Inkerman.

Lieutenant Curtis was killed in action in May 1955, struck by a round shot which also killed Lieutenant Carter of the Royal Engineers. His was the only death from enemy action amongst the officers, and O'Toole was the only other death.

Lieutenants, later Captains, Fane, Lluellyn, Forde and Dunscombe; Ensigns, later Lieutenants A.H. Waldy, Coote, Hammond, Hutton and Lawson; and Assistant-Surgeon Dempster, all served in the trenches. Lieutenant, later Captain, Hesketh served briefly but then left the regiment. The forgetful William Waldy, severely reprimanded, also served in Crimea.

Paymaster Alexis Corcoran went on half pay in August 1854 - perhaps no longer *persona grata* in the regiment?

Interestingly, six of the regiment's officers kept journals, sent home letters which were preserved, or later wrote books. Colonel Garrett kept a diary very briefly and nothing worthwhile survives. Captain Campbell, later Lieutenant Colonel, wrote letters home which were collected and published in 1894[164]. The 'forgetful' Lieutenant William Waldy published his reminiscences in 1914[165] but although he writes that, as a subaltern in Dublin, ragging and drinking were very prevalent in the mess, there is no mention of life at Windsor, nor of the events which led to the courts-martial. No doubt he had forgotten...

In recent times, two journals were edited by the present writer, that of Captain Richard Lluellyn published in 1994[166], and Captain Dunscombe's in 2003[167]. The letters of Major Dallas were edited by Michael Hargreave Mawson, a descendant, and were published in 2001[168]. None of these memoirs even mentions the events in Windsor in the summer of 1854.

Finally, what of the man thought by *The Times* and most of the population to be the real villain of the case, the commanding officer Robert Garrett? As mentioned earlier, he was a Peninsula veteran, indeed he had purchased an ensigncy in the 2nd Queen's Royal Regiment on 6 March 1811 and fought at Fuentes d'Onoro on May 5 that year. On 22 July 1812 in the battle of Salamanca he was wounded in head and hip in command of the Light Company

---

[164] *Letters from Sevastopol, 1854-5,* pub Bentley, London.

[165] *From Eight to Eighty,* pub London, Harrison.

[166] *The Murder of a Regiment,* pub Bowdon, Withycut House.

[167] *Captain Dunscombe's Diary: the real Crimean War,* pub Bowdon, Withycut House.

[168] *Eye Witness in the Crimea,* pub London, Greenhill. A very comprehensive account of the war which is highly recommended.

in the Storming Party at the attack on Centre Fort. He was appointed Lieutenant, without purchase, in the 2nd Garrison Battalion on 3 September 1812 and the following month moved to the 7th Royal Fusiliers. He was with them on 21 June 1813 at the battle of Vittoria and again at Sauroren, one of the so-called Pyrenees battles, from 26 July to 1 August 1813 as Marshal Soult, hugely outnumbering the British force, tried desperately to get back into Spain and suffered heavy losses. Amongst the British army, which also incurred heavy casualties, the 7th were the greatest sufferers and Garrett himself was severely wounded. He received the Peninsular medal with clasps for Fuentes d'Onoro, Salamanca, Vittoria and Pyrenees. He purchased a Captaincy in the 97th (later 96th) Queen's Own Germans on 7 July 1814 and went on half pay on that regiment's disbandment on 25 December 1818. He returned to the Active List as Captain with the 20th Foot on 8 June 1826 and shortly afterwards, on 19 September, purchased an unattached majority. On 7 February 1834 he exchanged to the 46th. In 1836 he was appointed Knight of the Royal Hanoverian Guelphic Order, instituted after Waterloo in 1815 and with its post-nominal letters 'K.H'. He was promoted Brevet Lieutenant Colonel in the army on 23 November 1841 and on 16 May 1845 purchased his lieutenant colonelcy in the 46th. He had taken his regiment out to the scene of war after the courts-martial. After Inkerman, and the many casualties in senior officers in that battle, Garrett's seniority as a Peninsular War veteran - he had been promoted Brevet Colonel in June 1854 - eventually led to him being appointed temporarily to command the Second Brigade of the 4th Division on 9th November 1854, but he was not appointed Local Brigadier General (Brigadier General was not then a rank, but merely an 'appointment') until 30 July 1855, and was confirmed as such in September 1855 when he temporarily took command of the 2nd Division. In October 1855 he was given Local Rank of 'Major General in Turkey' and in November 1855 he was appointed to command the 4th Division. Apart from minor

French and Turkish medals, he was not honoured as most of the other senior officers were after the conclusion of hostilities. In March 1856 there was a rumour in the regiment that he was to receive the K.C.B. (Knight Commander of the Order of the Bath) but he was overlooked until January 1857 - perhaps a deliberate mark of official displeasure for the widespread opprobium that the courts-martial had brought him and the British Army generally. Appointed Temporary Major General on 24 July 1856, he served in China in 1857 and then in India during the Mutiny where he commanded a division. He does not appear to have been highly rated by the Commander-in-Chief in India, Sir Colin Campbell, later Lord Clyde, who as an officer of very limited means cannot have looked with any sympathy on the conduct of the 46th before the Crimean War. On 20 October 1858 he was at last promoted Major General. He later commanded a District in the United Kingdom and was made Honorary Colonel of the 4th West India Regiment on 1 April 1862, and the 43rd Light Infantry on 14 January 1866. He was promoted Lieutenant General in March 1866 and died in June 1869, aged 75. He had triumphed in the end...

Appendix A - Perry's Defence Statement in his Second Trial

" Mr. President and Gentlemen of the court-martial, Borne down with fatigue and anxiety, I am now called upon to defend myself before this tribunal, not against clear, open, and written charges only, but against vague insinuations, which hostile and vindictive witnesses have thought fit to invent for the purpose of tarnishing my reputation and prejudging me before this Court and the public; but, nevertheless, I cheerfully rise in my own vindication, because I am persuaded that I shall meet with a continuance of that patience which has hitherto been so generously displayed by the Court, and because I know I shall meet with sympathy and justice at the hands of my gallant and honourable military judges. If I had not been supported during these protracted and harassing proceedings by a consciousness of innocence, I should long since have sunk exhausted, humiliated, and disgraced ; but, with conscious rectitude, I have, as a subaltern, been enabled to sustain this unequal contest, with only one friend to cheer, to advise, and to encourage me. With all the unkindness which has been exhibited by the witnesses for the prosecution, I am sure you will believe that all that could be has been said against me. It is not to vindictive slanders and calumnies on my reputation without foundation and support only that I have been subjected before this Court, but I have had to contend with concert, prearrangement of evidence, and conspiracy. When Lieutenant Dunscombe is asked whether, since that inquiry was instituted, and it was known that he would be called upon to give evidence, he had been spoken to relative to the nature of the evidence he would give, and who spoke to him, and what they said, he declined to answer the question. How many more witnesses for the prosecution have confessed to discussing the evidence to be given and declined to give the names of the parties with whom they so discussed it ! How many answers are given in the same stereotyped phraseology ! Are not these proofs of concert and prearrangement of evidence, for, if there had been no concert or prearrangement to conceal, why were not all my questions frankly answered? Again, I say I have to contend with a conspiracy in the regiment against me. After the letter on which the two first charges are founded was sent to the President of the court-martial on Lieutenant Greer, Colonel Garrett called the officers together, and, as they were anxious as far as possible to clear the colonel and vindicate themselves, they signed each of them papers, answering certain questions in reference to my letter, on the supposition that the Horse Guards would thereby be satisfied and the colonel relieved from further censure, little anticipating at that time that I should be the object of another inquiry. When a second court-martial was ordered upon me these volunteers of ignorance to the Horse Guards are called upon to give evidence. They have already committed themselves in their written answers. How is the difficulty to be overcome ? Simply enough. Only speak to the best of your recollection - *non mi recordo* - and the problem is solved. The difficulty is got over, but I am the victim. If there had been no conspiracy, why did Lieutenant Curtis, a relative, I believe, of the Colonel, state, first, that the officers did not assemble, and, when pressed if the officers were not in deliberation an hour, say that the meeting was for auditing the mess accounts. Whereas Lieutenant Hesketh says the officers were assembled simply to discuss what appeared in my letter, and the mess accounts were never audited on that occasion. Will any member of this Court give credit to the witnesses called for the prosecution - that the evidence from time to time was not duly discussed, and every hole made by me attempted to be stopped by answers stereotyped and arranged, till, driven to desperation, they personally attacked my private character by malignant falsehood, and what pretended ignorance and want of recollection could not effect was sought to be attained by calumny as mean as it was malicious? I feel persuaded that, as a young officer, without a father or relative to sustain or advise him while compelled to defend himself almost help. less and alone against charges so grave and numerous, I shall bespeak the manly and generous sympathy of every member of the Court; and when it is shown that I have been attacked and surrounded by conspiracy, combination, calumny, and perjury, may I not ask for more than sympathy - for a speedy and honourable acquittal ? I could have wished that the questions with respect to the prosecution had been confined simply to the charges against me, and that I had been spared the pain of hearing from my witnesses, who have been treated by me as sincere and faithful friends, the paltry reasons for shunning me. I feel it but just to myself to mention that my case has been injured in consequence of my being from time to time stopped in my cross-examination of witnesses when I was following out and exposing a vein of prevarication or some ramifications of falsehood or malice, and told by the Court that I could call such witnesses in my defence, as if it were in my power to break down, by an examination in chief a hostile witness in the same manner as by a sifting cross-examination. I am sure this Court, as soldiers, were not aware at the time of the difficulties such a course would entail on me. And I submit that I have another just cause of complaint, for when I sought for the production of Lieutenant Shervinton's letter, to shake the testimony of Captain Campbell, and to prove that I was not actuated by any desire to set at nought authority or to disparage my superiors, and that what he referred to was a mere jest, and had throughout been so treated by Lieutenant

Shervinton, the whole of the letters were carefully brought out, put upon record, and published, as if I bad been on my trial for every peccadillo of my life. With the exceptions just referred to, I am bound in justice to this Court to observe that I have been treated with great forbearance, kindness, and consideration. The course pursued by the President will ever entitle him to my warmest respect and gratitude, for never did I witness more dignity combined with justice, uprightness, and kindness. The observations that I have felt due to myself, in reference to the proceedings of this Court, I am sure will not be allowed by so gallant and honourable a body to militate against me. Nor will military *esprit de corps* be permitted to enter prejudicially into the bosoms of those who sit here as judges either to consign me to disgrace and infamy or by their verdict to pronounce me an injured and an innocent man. It will now become my painful duty to refer more particularly to the charges made against me, and the evidence by which those charges are attempted to be supported; after which I shall endeavour to analyze and criticize and show the worthlessness of that evidence. The charges made against me are, in substance, the following :

"1. That I falsely stated in a letter to Colonel Upton that Colonel Garrett reproached and called me a fool for my pains after I had reported to him.

" 2. That it was false that I made any threat to Colonel Garrett, either by word of mouth or in writing, that I would appeal to the General of the district.

" 3. That I stated falsely, in my evidence on Lieutenant Greer's trial, that Captain Nicholas had illtreated other officers on joining.

"4. That in my letter to Colonel Pipon, the Deputy-JudgeAdvocate on Mr. Greer's court-martial, I had falsely imputed to Captain Nicholas that he illtreated young officers, or aided and abetted others in doing so.

The first witness called on the first and second charges is Colonel Garrett, who stated that he does not remember the particular cause of my complaint to him, but thinks it had reference to pulling my bed about ; and that he had no recollection of having on that or on any other occasion reproached me and called me a fool for my pains. But when pressed, in cross-examination, distinctly to deny that he ever used the words in the presence of any one, says, in a most qualified manner, ' I really don't think I ever did; it is a long time ago; I cannot charge my memory with ever having made that observation.' And when subsequently asked if he had in any instance used reproachful language to any of the officers, after a complaint of being pulled out of bed, begs to decline answering the question. When again asked if he recollected, or whether the acting adjutant told him, that I threatened to report the circumstances to the General of the district, he said, ' I do not recollect.' The next witness examined for the prosecution, on the first and second charges, was Major Maxwell. When asked whether it was within his knowledge, or had he any reason to believe, that Colonel Garrett did call me a fool for my pains, or reproach me for making a complaint, he says be never heard Colonel Garrett call me a fool for my pains, and never heard Colonel Garrett reproach me for making a complaint. And in a subsequent part of his evidence he speaks of the severity of the reprimand given to the officers of whom I complained, and that the reprimand was so strong that the only instance of a practical joke that he knew of afterwards was that of Lieutenant Dunscombe; yet, so defective is the memory of Major Maxwell, that, although he could recollect Dunscombe's business in 1853, and recollects Dunscombe's appeal 'Major, will you stand this?' still he knew not afterwards of any instance of an officer being pulled out of his bed at Weedon, although that occurred only in the month of May last. But when further pressed as to an officer being brought down in his shirt, and placed on the table, he savs - 'I have some slight memory, of something of the kind happening at Weedon, but it made no impression on my mind at the time.' And this witness, in his evidence relating to Dunscombe's affair, would have led the Court to believe that all was settled amicably, for he says that Mr. Dunscombe appeared in his uniform in the ante-room about five minutes afterwards, although it is proved by Lieutenant Dunscombe and Major Fyffe that Lieutenant Dunscombe threatened by letter to appeal to the General of the district the following morning. The next witness for the prosecution is Major Fyffe, who, when asked by the prosecutor whether it was within his knowledge that Colonel Garrett did, on the occasion of my making a complaint, or on any other occasion, call me a fool for my pains, or reprove me for making complaints, stated certainly not, within his knowledge, nor did he ever hear that Colonel Garrett had so done. And when asked if he knew that I had ever sent a letter to Colonel Garrett threatening to appeal to the General of the district, stated he never heard of such a threat, either by letter or word, but that Colonel Garrett might have received such a letter without his knowledge. And subsequently, after great hesitation and several equivocations, he said he had heard in casual conversation that Lieutenant Dunscombe had complained to the General of the district by letter. I next come to Captain Sandwith, who so discreditably attempted to assail my private character, and who appears to have some enormous feeling of prejudice against me. He never heard Colonel Garrett call me a fool, or reproach me for making complaints. He does not know that I threatened to complain to the General of the district. He does not know that 1 ever was persecuted. This witness, who was adjutant, stated. that no system of persecution could have existed without his knowledge, yet it appeared, subsequently, by his evidence, that the persecution of Waldy and Knapp took place without his knowledge, and he afterwards boldly stared that Lieutenant Dunscombe's letter was not to the General of the district, but to the colonel only, whereas Lieutenant Dunscombe and Major Fyffe both proved that it was, through the colonel, to the General of the district. This evidence is therefore worse than useless. The next witness called against me is Captain Nicholas. He never heard me called a fool for my pains by Colonel Garrett, or reproached for reporting. He never beard that I threatened by letter to appeal to the General of the district. Lieutenant and Adjutant M'Alister is then called. He has no recollection of being present when an officer was reprimanded, never heard me called a fool for my pains. Never did I, to his knowledge, threaten to appeal to the General of the district. When, however, asked questions in reference to Dunscombe's affair, he heard that Colonel Garrett had not reprimanded him for making the complaint, but for improperly wording it, whereas Lieutenant Dunscombe says that he was blamed by the colonel for making a threat before applying to him. Lieutenant Dunscombe is the next witness against me, but I shall forbear making any further observation on his evidence beyond stating that when asked in cross-examination whether since this inquiry was instituted, and it was known he would be called as a witness, he h'ad been spoken to relative to the nature of the evidence he should give, and if so, by whom, and what did they say, he replied, 'I decline to answer the question;' but the effect of this pre-concert with the witness is remarkable, for when asked if since the regiment left Dublin he had been annoyed by the officers forcing their way into his room and pulling him out of his bed, be replied, 'I have by the prisoner himself, at Manchester;' and, when urged upon the point, admits that he was not even pulled out of his bed, but that his door was broken open, and he believed that I did it; as if it were possible for him to depose under the circumstances, to such a fact. The next witness against me is Lieutenant Curtis, a relative, I believe, of Colonel Garrett. Now, he speaks most strongly on the first charge, and he states positively that Colonel Garrett never reproached me for making a complaint, or called me a fool for my pains, and he does not know that I ever sent a letter to Colonel Garrett, threatening to appeal to the General of the district. This witness's evidence, however, is not entitled to either weight or credit, for when asked if the officers' assembly was not sounded, and if all the officers were not called together to refresh each other's memory,- he stated at first 'Certainly not!' and if the officers' assembly was sounded for any other purpose, he was not there. But, on re-consideration, be said he thought the officers' assembly did sound, but he had forgotten the day; it was for auditing the mess accounts that the assembly was sounded, and that the meeting was a day or two before the court-martial assembled - the day Colonel Garrett went to the Horse

Guards. Now, Lieutenant Hesketh expressly denies this, and says that the officers were assembled simply to discuss what appeared in my letter. This witness, however, does not deny he said to me, that ' I think you got the worst of reporting this time, old fellow;' and, again, although this witness did not recollect Colonel Garrett calling me a fool for my pains, an independent witness, Captain Chambers, has sworn that he told him that Colonel Garrett had called me a fool for my pains for reporting, and that the circumstance was referred to by several officers of the mess. Colonel Garrett is again called in reference to the second charge, and says he never received any letter threatening to complain to the General of the district, although he positively stated that be did not recollect; but when asked if he had no clearer recollection of my letter to him than he had of calling me a fool for my pains, and if I proved he was in error when he said he did not call me a fool for my pains, would he not think himself equally in error when he said I did not write him the letter, he replied that if it should be proved that he was mistaken on either one or other of these points it would be for the Court, but not for himself, to pass its own opinion. Still there is no great confidence in Colonel

Garrett's recollection, and be admits that if in error in one case he may be in the other. The next witness is Lieutenant Hesketh, whose evidence amounts to nothing against me. He was not present when the reprimand was given. He does not know whether Colonel Garrett called me a fool for my pains, and he never heard that I had written to Colonel Garrett threatening to complain to the General of the district. The effect of all which evidence on the first charge is, that Colonel Garrett does not recollect calling me a fool for my pains; Major Maxwell never heard him say so; Major Fyffe had no knowledge of it; Captain Sandwith never heard it; Captain Nicholas never heard it; Lieutenant and Adjutant M'Alister never heard it, and Lieutenant Hesketh never heard it. There are, therefore, eight witnesses, all of whom state they either did not hear Colonel Garrett call me a fool for my pains, or did not recollect Colonel Garrett calling me a fool for my pains. Two witnesses, Lieutenants Dunscombe and Curtis, speak more distinctly, but, for the reasons before stated, their evidence is less than worthless. The first charge therefore, on the evidence brought to support it, has positively failed. My statement is an affirmative statement, and is not only true in fact, but in law is presumed to be true until its falsehood is shown. But no quantity of *non mi ricordo* evidence can amount to proof. No accumulation of nothings can produce an unit, for it is perfectly consistent with my statement that all the eight witnesses may neither not have recollected nor have heard Colonel Garrett call me a fool, and still be may have called, and did call me a fool, notwithstanding.

I come now to a summary of the prosecutor's evidence on the second charge. Colonel Garrett says he never did receive my letter threatening to complain to the General of the district, having previously stated that he had no recollection of the circumstance; Major Maxwell gave no evidence on the point; Major Fyffe never heard of my so doing; Captain Sandwith does not know of my so doing; Captain Nicholas never heard of my so doing; Lieutenant and Adjutant M'Alister had no knowledge of my so doing; Lieutenant Dunscombe has no knowledge of my so doing; Lieutenant Curtis has no knowledge of my so doing; Lieutenant Hesketh has never heard of my so doing; so that, in fact, the only witness who attempts to prove by any shadow of legal evidence the second charge is Colonel Garrett.

I proceed now to the evidence produced on thepart of the prosecutor to the third and fourth charges. Sixteen witnesses have been called with the intention to prove a negative to support those charges. Ensign Coots in his evidence denies that Captain Nicholas on any occasion called him 'a d-----d son of a b----h of an ensign,' but Lieutenant Waldy shows that those opprobrious epithets were applied by Captain Nicholas to the witness. Ensign Hutton does not remember ever having heard Captain Nicholas use opprobrious language towards young officers. Lieutenant W. T. Waldy, though he denies that he ever said or even wrote that Captain Nicholas called Ensign Coote 'a d---d son of a b----h of an ensign,' is convicted by his own letter of having prevaricated, for in that letter, written immediately after the occurrence, he expressly says that Captain Nicholas did use those opprobrious words to Ensign Coote at the mess table, and that he never saw such fun; the evidence therefore of Lieutenant W.T. Waldy and Ensign Coote is rendered worthless, and the evidence of Ensign Hutton, who only deals in a *non mi ricordo* relative to Captain Nicholas's opprobrious language, does net, therefore, support either the third or fourth charges made against me. Lieutenant Dunscombe, when asked if he ever heard Captain Nicholas use opprobrious language to him for reporting, replies, `Never to my recollection;' and when asked whether Captain Nicholas was not present when he (Dunscombe) was pulled out of his bed by Captain Webb, made the qualified reply, `I do not remember that he was.' When again asked, if any officer ever stated to him or in his presence that he would be revenged for indignities heaped upon him by Captain Nicholas, he replied, ' Never to any recollection;' and when again asked who the officers were of whom he complained, he said there were four, but he only recollected Greer and Knapp; and I when further pressed as to who the other two were, he said, ' Captain Nicholas was not one of them.' Now, how is it possible for Lieutenant Dunscombe to say that Captain Nicholas was not one of those officers when he declares he does not recollect who they were? He subsequently, however, endeavours to account for recollecting Greer and

Knapp, only because Knapp was in Turkey and Greer under arrest, and his answer is very remarkable, for he says the very circumstance of one being in Turkey and the other being under arrest served to impress their names on his memory. Now, will any reasonable man believe that an *ex post facto* circumstance would serve to impress the names of two of the parties on the memory of this witness, and yet that he should still continue oblivious as to the rest? Lieutenant Ford is then called, but exhibits total want of memory, for when asked whether Curtis and Fane were not in his room when he was pulled out of bed by Ensign Castles of the 17th, he stated that there was only one officer of the 46th there, and that was Lieutenant Greer, and that, upon his attempting to lay hold of his bedclothes, he caught hold of him and thrust him out of the room; but on reference to Lieutenant Curtis's evidence, it will be found that he states that he and two other officers of the 46th were present, and that Ford thrust, not Greer, but Ensign Castles out of the room, and, as Lieutenant Curtis immediately succeeded Lieutenant Ford, and had not an opportunity of' looking into the newspapers and seeing what that witness stated, he no doubt, in this instance, spoke the truth. Lieutenant Curtis appears only to be remarkably forgetful, for when examined on the third and fourth charges, upon which he speaks strongly, be admits that, on alleging, when he last gave his evidence, that the meeting of the ofiicors to canvas my letter was merely to audit the mess accounts, he totally forgot such meeting had been held. How is it possible that any weight can be given to the testimony of such a witness, when he forgets so momentous a meeting as that which was held, and attempts to substitute for it a meeting for auditing the mess accounts, which it was afterwards proved never took place at all ? I will not trouble the Court further as to the prevarication of this witness on the third and fourth charges. Lieutenant Lluellyn is then called; he simply says that he had never seen or heard that Captain Nicholas aided and abetted in the annoying of young officers, and, when asked whether Captain Nicholas had any hand in throwing the things out of Knapp's and Waldy's room, said he had not, to the best of his recollection. When again asked how many officers assisted he says, to the best of his recollection, he only remembered one; but when pressed with a question that detailed an amount of work that would have occupied a number of men for a considerable time, he answers that he thinks there were some officers in Waldy's room, but he only recollects himself being engaged in throwing things out of the window, although Captain Chambers states that he was the person who threw the things out of the window, and that he (Captain Chambers) took them back again. Lieutenant Fane, when examined and asked if he ever heard Captain Nicholas use opprobrious language to any other officer, replied, not to his knowledge. The next witness examined is Lieutenant Greer (whom I heartily forgive for his treatment of me, and on whose account, indirectly, I am now in my present situarion), and he speaks with a degree of positiveness to all that tells against me; but when I asked him if he did not say quite recently to an officer who is now gone to Turkey that I had been an illtreated and badly-used man ever since I joined the regiment, he replied, 'I have no recollection of i ;' and, when further questioned, states that he had discussed the nature of the evidence given with one or two officers of the regiment, but, when strongly pressed, thinks there were six or seven officers with him, but declines to mention their names; and, when asked if Lieutenant Shervinton had been authorized by him to deliver any message to me, said he did not recollect authorizing him to deliver any message to me. It will be observed that to every important question that was put to this witness that would tend to my benefit and support my case, he replied by ` *Non mi ricordo.'* Lieutenant and Adjutant M'Alister, when examined against me on these charges, simply says that he was not aware that Captain Nicholas aided and abetted in annoying young officers, as if that evidence, which is equivalent to a *non mi ricordo,* is sufficient to prove the falseness of my statement. Captain Campbell is the next witness examined, bur, with all his injustice towards me, and with all his desire to produce an unfavourable impression against me, he does not attempt to say more than this, that Captain Nicholas does not aid or abet others in annoying young officers, to the best of his belief ; but, when pressed by n:e with this question, `Have you never heard of any practical jokes in which Captain Nicholas has been concerned?' replied, - and may I beg you to mark the reply? - ' A practical joke is a wide term; I have never known him join in a practical joke to annoy any one.' To the rest of Captain Colin Campbell's evidence I will not refer; but this I will declare, that the attempt on the part of the prosecutor to produce a series of letters containing charges against me that had been condoned, forgiven, and forgotten was an act of injustice I little expected at his hands, and the attempt of Captain Campbell to neutralize the effect of Lieutenant Shervinton's generous admission, 'that, as well when he reported as afterwards, he was always of opinion that I acted in a thoughtless and inconsiderate manner, without the most distant intention of showing contempt for authority or committing a breach of discipline,' is as mean as it is malicious. Out of 16 witnesses who were called to prove the third and fourth charges seven I have convicted of prevarication. Two others of them, when asked as to opprobrious language used by Captain Nicholas, simply answered *'Non mi ricordo.'* Another answers that he was not aware; and Captain Campbell does not deny the participation of Captain Nicholas in practical jokes. The rest are so young in the service I never knew them until I came to Windsor. Can such evidence as this be relied upon as a logical and legal proof of Captain Nicholas never having illtreated brother-officers? There was a clearer and more distinct, a more definite mode of proof, and the only positive, moral, and legal proof to support the third and fourth charges, and that was the evidence of Captain Nicholas himself. Colonel Garrett, who was immediately affected by the first and second charges, was examined by the prosecutor in support of those charges, and why was notCaptain 'Nicholas examined to support the third and fourth charges? Because the practical jokes referred to by Captain Campbell, the aiding and abetting of which Lieutenant M'Adister was not aware of, and the opprobrious language so many did not recollect, but which was in one instance, unfortunately for the prosecution, committed to writing, would all have been made manifest, and myself vindicated, and Captain Nicholas shown to have illtreated other officers on joining. I have now dissected the evidence given on the part of the prosecution in support of all the charges against me, and I venture to assert, as I am told by the highest legal authorities, that on such evidence no civil judge or jury of my country would hesitate a moment to find me innocent of all the charges laid against me; and I am confident that, when you shall have weighed the evidence and observed the *anirnus* of the witnesses, with the concert and conspiracy to crush me, you will, even on the case as made out by the prosecution, unanimously find me not guilty. I will now proceed further to trespass upon the patience of this honourable tribunal by referring to the indnignities I received at the hands of my brother officers, which I was ultimately induced to resent, and which has ended in this inquiry. When I first joined the 46th I was 20 years of age. It was on the 14th of April, 1853, that I came fresh from my tutor to the barracks. My father was then serving his country as an officer in the Royal Irish Fusileers, in India. I had no friends nor near relations who were interested in me ; and I was placed in the regiment to fight my own way in the world, with the limited pay of an ensign, and such slight pecuniary assistance as my father could afford me out of his pay. As officers, you must see that I was not a rich man. I had none of the advantages which wealth commands, and was therefore unable to support the character of a fast man consistently with that of an honourable one. On the contrary, I was necessarily debarred from many pleasures and many comforts which I gladly saw others enjoy. My time I however occupied not in low debauchery, not in drunkenness and riot, not in disturbing the comfort and wounding the feelings of my brother officers by practical jokes, as some have endeavoured to insinuate, but in the study of my profession; and during the short period I have been in the regiment I have rendered myself tolerably conversant with fortifications and other branches of the service. I have occupied my leisure hours chiefly in the improvement of my mind, and in the cultivation of music, drawing, and the modern languages; and I did look forward to the time when I might have served my Queen as a brave and able officer. No sooner had I joined the regiment than I became the object of continued indignities and annoyances. I was pulled out of my bed, and on many occassions made to go through the sword exercise in a state of nudity. My shirt was torn from my back; I was beaten with an umbrella; I was compelled by force to get into my tub; and these indignities were practised upon me, not merely in the presence of officers, but privates in the regiment were witnesses of the proceedings. I experienced for some time these degradations, and asked the advice of an old officer, who told me to put up with such treatment as well as I could until younger officers joined, when I should be relieved. I was not, however, relieved, and I at last complained to officers of the regiment - to Major Maxwell, and even to my commanding officer, and met with no redress. I would cheerfully have submitted to any fair share of annoyance; but there is a limit to human forbearance, and to the forbearance of a friendless subaltern. On the last occasion which occurred I dressed in full uniform, and came down beween 2 and 3 in the morning, insisting on seeing Colonel Garrett, when I was met in the passage, and threatened even with personal violence if I reported, and I was prevented from entering the room in which the colonel and others were regaling themse:ves. I sent in a written letter, through the colonel, to the general of the district, reporting the conduct of the officer towards me, the next day. He called me a d-----d fool for reporting anything to my commanding officer, and added, I was just like a child escaped from my mothers apron strings. But I was earnestly entreated by several of my brother officers to forbear; and I was asked by Colonel Garrett if I wished the letter to go before the general; and I replied, I did not wish to ruin any man's prospects, and would be satisfied if Colonel Garrett would give him such a reprimand as would cause all future annoyance to cease. I consulted, on many occasions, with Paymaster Corcoran. He advised me to put up with the indignities, and pointed out the course I should pursue in applying to the general of the district. And when I found that the complain:t to my commanding officer was treated with scorn, and I was called a fool for my pains, and likened unto a child escaped from his mother's apron strings, I felt overwhelmed, and went immediately to Mr.Corcoran, and told him the reception I had met with from Colonel Garrett, how I had threatened to report to the general of the district, and how I had consented to forbear. Ever since my determination to resist the personal attack upon me became known, I have been treated with coolness, and my society shunned. I became a marked man thenceforth. After repeated acts of violence by the officers of the 46th, I reported the circumstance to Colonel Garrett, and through him to the general of the district; he reproached me, and called me a fool for my pains; and Colonel Garrett gave the offenders so weak a reprimand, that, although the acts of aggression were discontinued, I was persecuted in other ways. On the 29th day of June last the unfortunate affair with Lieutenant Greer took place. I felt myself to be innocent; still I was tried first, and had to take the whole force of public opinion upon myself, until I was enabled to vindicate - nay, justify myself. Although I was, on my trial, prevented from procuring, from adverse witnesses, the evidence necessary to my defence, and this opinion was confirmed by the Deputy Judge-Advocate General, my trial was closed. Lieutenant Greer was afterwards tried. I was compelled to give evidence against him. I did so : I spoke nothing but the truth. The other evidence, however, called on Lieutenant Greer's trial was thought by a legal friend of mine from Ireland, who was present, to be produced more to criminate me than support the prosecution; and he called, in a state of considerable indignation on my solicitor, Mr. Darvill, and urged that a letter should be written to the President of the Court-Martial. You have already heard how that letter was written and how it came into the public journals. The statements in that letter are, however, substantially true and, although I was not morally responsible for its contents and never read it, I signed it at the request of my friend, who delivered it to Colonel Upton. I do not seek by any mean subterfuge either to avoid the substance or the consequences of that letter, for although the letter is not literally correct in the precise narrative of the circumstances, it would have been more correct if it had stated what I have previously said about Colonel Garrett calling me a fool for my pains. I have now stated how the causes of the first and second charges against me arose. As to the third charge, I have only again to state that the evidence I gave on Lieutenant's Greer's trial was true, and nothing but the truth; and the statements for which I am now tried were extracted from me rather than volunteered by me. As to the fourth charge, I wish only to observe that the letter to LieutenantColonel Pipon, which is the basis of the fourth charge against me, was written as a privileged communication and is unfairly used against me, On my first trial, Major Pack, the Deputy Judge.Advocate, called on me. and told me he was as much my adviser as the adviser of the Court; and I thought of course that Colonel Pipon, as Deputy Judge Advocate on the second court-martial, was also my adviser, and therefore wrote to him, in consequence of the unfair course adopted in the endeavour to criminate me on a trial in which I was not the prisoner. That letter, however, I see no occasion to retract, nor do I seek to retract it. I now come to the evidence called in my defence. It was not in my power to produce any evidence in the regiment on which I could confidently rely. My brother officers were committed; and their independence as witnesses was lost to me. Captains O'Toole and Hardy, and Lieutenants Shervinton and Knapp are in Turkey. Ensign Stretton is in the service of the Ottoman Porte. Mr. Leonard, late of the 46th Regiment, was seized with diarrhoea in Ireland, and could not come. To ascertain why those witnesses left, I have carefully gone through the states of all the companies in the regiment on the 14th of July last, the day the two companies left for Turkey.

The regulations direct that companies for service shall be taken from the senior captains downwards. Now, it is somewhat remarkable that in the present instance this regulation should have been departed from, and that that departure should have removed from me some most important witnesses. The senior company was on detachment at Kensington. The next company (Captain Wombwell's) had 41 men on detachment, and therefore could not have been expected to embark for Turkey. The next company (Captain O'Toole's) were all at head-quarters. The next three companies in succession of seniority were Captain Campbell's, Captain Garrett's, and Captain Piper's, each of which have only 1 officer, 1 sergeant, and I private on detachment; so that they were ready and fit to embark, yet still they were passed over, and Captain Hardy's company taken, in which were two of my most important witnesses - Captain Hardy and Lieutenant Shervinton. I do not say that this partial and unexplained selection, contrary to the regulations, was intentional ; but I do say it was suspicious and has lost me the aid of much valuable evidence; and it is somewhat remarkable that Lieutenant Shervinton, the senior lieutenant, should have been attached to a company the captain of which was his junior in the service. If, however, I have not been fortunate enough to secure the attendance of those officers of my regiment who would have befriended me by honest and unbiased testimony, I have produced before you witnesses so uninfluenced and unprejudiced that their evidence is above suspicion; and I have opposed to all the *non mi recordo* evidence of the prosecutor the evidence of witnesses whose moral testimony is unanswerable. Paymaster Corcoran, who is as free from the influence as he is above the corruption of my opponents, has given evidence which leaves with it the impress of perfect truthfulness. He speaks to facts which could not have been concerted; he states what took place in May, 1853, when no one could have anticipated this inquiry. He has shown them that he was acquainted with my persecution, that he gave me advice and told me how to act, and that he advised me to write through the colonel to the general of the district, and that I told him I had done so; and that I went to him the following morning, much excited and in tears, and told him that I had reported certain officers to Colonel Garrett, and that he had called me a fool for so doing, and that I was like a child escaped from my mother's apron. strings. Could all this have been invented by so staid and respectable a witness for this occasion ? Could I have invented it in May, 1853, to meet the present purpose? But is not the evidence supported, not only by Captain Chambers, but also by the unwilling evidence of Lieutenant Curtis, who said he did not deny having said, ` I think you (meaning myself) have got the worst of reporting this time, old fellow.' Captain Chambers, now an officer with the Fourth West Yorkshire Militia, and a gentleman of considerable fortune, who was in the 46th, has given evidence, not only that Lieutenant Curtis told him that Colonel Garrett had called me a fool for my pains for reporting, but that the fact was openly spoken of among the officers. This evidence is above suspicion; and, if what he says be true, it shows that the truth has been suppressed by all the witnesses for the prosecution, which impresses the whole of the evidence against me with suspicion, if it does not stamp it with conspiracy and perjury. The evidence of Major Stuart shows that all the witnesses have not only been unjust towards me, but have strained that injustice into falsehood when they stated in their stereotyped answers, that I was shunned for my overbearing and swaggering manner. He also shows that redress for a subaltern in my situation, when complaining of personal annoyance, was hopeless, and that practical jokes were not repressed but encouraged, and were common in the regiment for many years. The witnesses called on my behalf have all spoken to nsy credit and my honour, and could not have done so had I been the infamous character represented by some of the prosecutor's witnesses ; who, in their zeal to crush me, proved too much when they endeavoured to blast my reputation and to create a prejudice against me. When I was accused of impertinent familiarity, it transpired that I had once, in kindly addressing a brother officer at the dinner-table called him by his Christian name. Then I was accused of supposed debauched habits, which turned out ultimately to have been simply a slander upon me. My disgusting conduct towards a friend of one witness was of so discreditable a character that the vindictive witness who asserted it was reluctantly compelled to acknowledge that his friend regarded the whole affair as a joke ; and when this witness discovered a general difficulty in keeping me within the bounds of discipline, it turns out that, while on leave at Cork, I had gone to Middleton, and had written to my servant, with directions either to get an extension of my leave or to give me notice of its refusal ; and that leave was given, and my attendance not required. This witness must have been sadly in need of breaches of discipline to have distorted so simple an occurrence to my disadvantage. These are my antecedents referred to by Colonel Garrett. Again, I was assailed by another witness for disgraceful conduct in a money transaction; and I appeal to this assembly of British officers, and I ask them whether the charge, so maliciously insinuated against me, was not as groundless as it was dishonourable? Although I have been assailed by vindictiveness and calumny beyond the charges made against me, I have exhibited an amount of forbearance in the disclosure I might have made, which ought to insure me the generous sympathy, at least of Colonel Garrett and many of the officers of my regiment. I have called no evidence on the third and fourth charges, although I could have maintained those charges by the evidence of absent witnesses; but I submit that the prosecutor's own witnesses have proved the statement made by me in reference to Captain Nicholas to be true, for Captain Campbell does not deny Captain Nicholas's participation in practical jokes, and Lieutenant Waldy proves the coarse and opprobrious expressions used by Captain Nicholas; for will any member of this Court believe that the expression at the end of that letter, ` I never saw such fun,' did not mean that Lieutenant Waldy was present and saw and heard what took place? And if, as he says in his letter, this took place at the mess, how can the witnesses for the prosecution be believed who state they never heard Captain Nicholas use opprobrious words towards any young officer? But, as I before observed, the evidence against me on the third and fourth charges simply amounts to no witness having recollected Captain Nicholas illtreating young officers, or aiding or abetting in so doing, but the glaring, obvious, and manifest defect in the prosecutor's evidence is, not the prevarication of his witness, but the suspicious absence of Captain Nicholas in support of the third and fourth charges. I must crave the patience of the Court for a few moments in drawing attention to three important features in the evidence for the prosecution. There are two circumstances which took place before many officers - one of them was the public conversation after mess of Colonel Garrett having called me a fool for reporting; another was the fact of Captain Nicholas having called Ensign Coote a ----- son of a bitch of an ensign at the mess. Now, all the witnesses for the prosecution deny having heard either of these subjects referred to, or profess not to have recollection of them. Now, I leave it to this Court to conceive how it was possible that such circumstances could have escaped the observation and the memory of so many men; and, in my case, is it not far more likely that my memory should be more accurate and retentive, when I was the subject of reproach and sought my only remedy ? Is not the one who receives a wound more likely to recollect it than he who, with carelessness and indifference, deals out the blow? The other fact to which I beg to draw attention is, that when my reputation was assailed by specific charges, I was able to refute them. I have refuted them, and I have, moreover, refuted the charge of being overbearing and swaggering in my manner. Many witnesses swore to my overbearing and swaggering manner, which is denied by Major Stuart; now, are they to be believed on other points to which they have attempted to speak? Again, there is another important circumstance. Colonel Garrett said that all the subalterns were assembled to hear the reprimand he gave to Lieutenant Curtis on my complaint ; yet it is very remarkable that only one subaltern has given evidence of his being present and having heard that reprimand, although there were 18 subalterns in the regiment at that time. Captain Chambers, who was then a lieutenant, has stated in evidence that he was told on that occasion he was not wanted; but where is the evidence of any one witness for the prosecution who attempts to say that Colonel Garrett did not use the opprobrious epithets towards me, or who has attempted to say I did not

205

write a letter to the General of the district in reference to the indignities I received, and who has attempted to say that Captain Nicholas never did illtreat young officers, or aid or abet in so doing ? Not one. I, therefore, under all the circumstances, respectfully submit that the case as attempted to be made out against me has failed, and has exhibited all the vindictiveness, preconcert, and perjury of which I complained when I first opened my defence. The case of the prosecutor is either sound in all the charges or sound in none. Falsehood on one charge contaminates all the evidence on every charge. I have felt great difficulty in the preparation of my defence, and only closed my own evidence yesterday; and I have found the amount of evidence before me so extensive and so diversified in its nature, character, and incident, so contradictory and inconsistent, and so tainted with vindictiveness, forgetfulness, and suppression of the truth, that I trust every allowance will be made for my feeble and inefficient defence. In forbearing to call distant witnesses, I have had regard to the public interests and to you, for I desired no longer to fatigue you with a prolonged and delayed consideration of my case. I have now done, and cast myself upon your sympathies and your love of truth and justice; for I solemnly declare, in the presence of this imposing assembly of British officers, and in the presence of my country and my final Judge, that I am innocent of the charges preferred against me; and I leave myself, my conduct, and my reputation in your hands, with a consciousness that you will do me justice; and may God defend the right!"

Appendix B - Wetherall's Memorandum of 2nd September 1854

INSTRUCTIONS &c.
MEMORANDUM

Horse Guards, 2nd September 1854.
1. The General Commanding-in-Chief had in the course of last year been twice under the necessity of expressing to every regiment at home and abroad his apprehensions that a few inconsiderate officers might bring their regiments into disrepute, unless, in their social conduct towards each other at their mess table and in their barrack rooms, their behaviour should be regulated by a higher standard of what is due to the honourable position in which they stand, as the holders of commissions in Her Majesty's army.

2. The first case which required Viscount Hardinge to assemble a court martial on any officer was that of the 50th Regiment, on which occasion, four subalterns were tried for forcibly seizing a young Ensign, taking him to a pump, and there pumping upon him.
Two of the offending officers were sentenced to be dismissed[169] the service, and two were reprimanded.
The Memorandum containing Viscount Hardinge's commitments was dated 5th July 1853, and was read to the officers assembled of every regiment in the service.[170]

---

[169] The two dismissed were Lieutenants Leeds a\nd Roberts.
[170] Not included here but summarized as follows: General Hardinge expressed the deepest concern at the disgusting and insulting language used to the victim and the way he had been treated in an instance of outrage unparalleled in the British army. It was clear that the offenders had acted in great excitement and

3. The second instance occurred in the 62nd Regiment in October 1853.

A Captain in command of two companies had repeatedly annoyed and disturbed the subaltern of his own company, and, accompanied by other officers, had been in the habit of bursting into his room, and taking his bed to pieces, &c. &c.

The Lieutenant had the proper spirit to make his report to the Major of his regiment.

The officer commanding the regiment did his duty firmly; he supported the subaltern, and reported his case to the Horse Guards.

The captain was removed to another regiment, and lost five steps towards his advancement. Another subaltern was also removed, and the other Captain was retained in the 62nd, at the intercession of the commanding officer, on account of his good services in the field in India.

The facts of the case, and the punishment awarded, were printed and circulated, and read to the officers of every regiment assembled.

4. A third instance has now occurred. It is that in the 46th Regiment. The case originated in a disgraceful scene of deep gambling in a barrack-room at Windsor, between Lieutenant Greer and Lieutenant Perry, terminating in a violent assault, in the course of which disgusting language was applied by Lieutenant Greer to Lieutenant Perry.

---

irritation and it was evident that the outrage could not be glossed over as being a mere practical joke carried too far. After the victim had sought an apology he had been violently pushed out of the room.

5. At the close of the trial of Lieutenant Greer a letter was handed in to the President of that court martial by Lieutenant Perry, charging his commanding officer, Colonel Garrett, with grave acts of injustice, and stating that he (Lieutenant Perry) had sent a letter to his commanding officer, threatening to appeal to the General officer of the district &c. &c. Colonel Garrett denied these acts of injustice imputed to him, and he denied that any such letter had ever been sent to him by Lieutenant Perry.

6. The General Commanding-in-Chief took the same course in this case as he had done in that of the 50th, and for the same reason, viz. his determination not to consent to a compromise in any of these cases, but to eradicate the unmanly system. The charges made by Lieutenant Perry against Colonel Garrett were specific. They amounted to a breach of Her Majesty's Regulations, and apparently were in defiance of the admonitions and orders circulated in July and December 1853.
The General Commanding-in-Chief resolved, therefore, that the truth or falsehood of these charges should be investigated by a court martial on oath.

7. The result of that court martial, as well as of the two preceding trials in the 46th Regiment, is given in the Appendix *(now in chronological order as Appendices F, D and E)*, in order that every young officer may have on his first joining his regiment, by means of these examples, a clear understanding of his own position. He will carefully read the Articles of War, given in the Appendix *(now in Appendix C2)*, together with a letter of the Judge Advocate General of 1844 *(now in Appendix C1)*, which was published to the army, with the Mutiny Act and Articles of War of that year.

If the Ensign is firm, and has the proper spirit of an officer and a gentleman, he can have no difficulty, without any loss of honour or of temper, in resisting coarse practical jokes.

But if he submits to them on the plea that they are the customary probation of an officer entering the British army, he will justly subject himself to the charge of having tamely submitted to insult; and it is his duty on every account, and especially for the purpose of ensuring, his military efficiency, which depends upon character, that he should not suffer any liberties to be taken, calculated to expose him to the derision of his brother officers, and the men under his command.

8. These coarse irregularities, termed practical jokes, and the use of disgusting language, have increased, it is said, since the introduction of those Articles of War in,1844, which more strictly prohibited duelling in the Army.

Public feeling had, in the preceding year, been greatly shocked by two officers, who were brothers-in-law, having fought a duel, in which one was killed.

The better and truer reason, however, for the increased strictness of the Articles prohibiting duelling was, that the tone of society had improved, and that all men were united in reprobating so barbarous a mode of settling a dispute.

A few men of coarse and ungenerous tempers, since the severer Articles of War have been published, may have sought to take advantage of the apparent impunity which the prohibition afforded, and have taken greater liberties with their brother officers than they did when under the apprehension of immediate personal consequences.

Such practices cannot be permitted; they must be repressed, for they are degrading to the character of an officer. They render him unfit to command his men, for they cannot feel for him the respect which is the basis of all enduring authority. They render him unfit to associate with his brother officers, who must hold him in contempt, or must have themselves sunk so low as not to shrink from contact with men of such coarse vulgarity.

It can never be endured that the manners of British officers shall fall below the standard recognized by gentlemen.

As far as duels were permitted at all, they were suffered as means supposed to be conducive to the end of maintaining in the barrack and messroom the language and behaviour of gentlemen.

But it would be a fatal mistake to infer that because duelling has been prohibited, any lower standard of manners will be tolerated in the British army. The language and behaviour which formerly were held to justify a challenge must now, therefore, be visited by the removal of the offender from the society of which he has shown himself to be an unworthy member.

9. Every assistance and support will be given to the young officer in his endeavours to avoid rendering himself liable to these consequences.

In May last, before the spring inspections, the General Officers and Staff Officers, inspecting regiments, were ordered to report 'whether any practical jokes have been carried on at the mess table,or elsewhere, or any steps taken to prevent them.'

The reports are satisfactory: few regiments, however, have been inspected, owing to the greater part of regiments having previously embarked for foreign service.

10. The Captain of the company to which the Ensign, on joining, is appointed, will give him advice and support.

The Major entrusted by the Commanding Officer with this branch of the interior discipline of a regiment will do the same, and be held responsible that he does it. effectually; and if any case should arise requiring interference or a reprimand, the terms of the reprimand and the record of the letters must be forthcoming, to be shown to the General Officer, and sent up to the Horse Guards.

The necessity is apparent after the recent trials in the 46th Regiment, and all serious cases will at once be reported to the Adjutant General, for the decision of the General Commanding-in-Chief.

11. No case of a practical joke appears to have occurred in the 46th Regiment since October 1853, with the exception of the case of Lieut. Dunscombe, 46th, at Weedon,. in 1854.

12. General Viscount Hardinge confidently asserts that the regimental system of the British army, now so long established, has proved its efficiency as being admirably adapted for all the varied duties of war and peace.

He trusts that the irregularities and mischievous tendencies resulting from practical jokes can and will disappear for ever.

A firm but temperate exercise of authority on the part of commanding officers of regiments will effect the object desired; they will find, by a faithful discharge of their duty, that they will obtain the respect and support of their officers, and the esteem of their fellow subjects.

By command of General VISCOUNT HARDINGE,
Commanding-in-Chief,

G. A. WETHERALL,
Deputy Adjutant General.

Appendix C1 - Judge Advocate's Letter re Duelling

Judge Advocate General's Office,　　　*20ᵗʰ March, 1844.*

Sir,
The recent discussions on Duelling in the Army, and the alterations in the Articles of War, have directed my attention to the language of charges, under which Officers alleged to have submitted to indignity and insult, or to the imputation of dishonourable or unworthy conduct, have been, in repeated instances, been brought to trial.

An erroneous notion has, to a limited extent, obtained, that an Officer can be brought to trial and punished for not challenging another, or for refusing to accept a challenge, or to fight a duel; and in charges upon which Officers have been cashiered, or otherwise punished, expressions may be found, which if detached from the context, and considered without reference to the undoubted law of England, and to the clear and unambiguous language of the Articles of War, might afford some colour to this error.

But it must be remembered, that by common law of England, dueling, unattended by any injury to either party, is an aggravated offence against the public peace, punishable by fine and imprisonment. Thus, Mr. Justice Blackstone says – 'The punishment of common affrays is by fine and imprisonment. Where two persons coolly and deliberately engage in a duel, this being attended with an apparent intention and danger of murder, and being a high contempt of the justice of the nation, is a strong aggravation of the affray, though no mischief has actually ensued.' Under a recent statute, such persons may become liable to transportation. If death ensues, the parties may be tried for murder.

The military code has been, and will continue consistent with this.

213

The 107th Article of War, 1844 renders all parties, principals as well as seconds, implicated in duelling, liable to be cashiered.

The 103 and 104th Articles prescribe to a commanding officer the duty of preserving order in his Regiment, and of placing under arrest all who use reproachful speeches and gestures; a duty enjoined, with the view of preventing duels, and of bringing to trial by Court Martial parties who offer insults, and who will not afford redress by apology and acknowledgment of their error. Moreover, Officers in command of guards are under the 60th Article punishable for allowing persons to go forth to fight a duel.

By the 104th Article Officers of inferior rank may place under arrest those who are engaged in quarrels, frays, or disorders; and by Articles 35 and 144 any Officer, though of superior rank, who refuses to obey, is liable to be cashiered; while in the 105th Article Her Majesty points out to the Army that those who, being willing to make or accept frank explanations, apologies or redress, refuse challenges, act as is suitable to the character of honourable men, do their duty as good soldiers, and are not only acquitted of all disgrace, but of all opinion of disadvantage.

It is manifest then that an officer cannot be subjected to trial and punishment for leaving undone that which the law thus expressly forbids, or for doing that which is thus distinctly declared not merely to be no offence, but to be suitable to the character of a man of honour, to be conformable to military duty, and to be conduct above all blame and reproach.

Still an officer who allows the stigma of dishonourable conduct to rest upon him, or passes, over, without notice,, an insult offered to him, is liable to be brought to trial before a Court Martial -- not because he declines to fight a duel, but because, having failed to obtain speedy atonement through the intervention of mutual friends, or by other lawful means, he neglects to report the matter to his commanding officer, and thereby to invite a searching investigation into his character and conduct. By such neglects he seems either to acquiesce in the justice of the imputation cast upon him, and to admit that there is something in his conduct which he fears to lay bare before honourable men, or to show that, regardless of his own reputation and honour, he knows not what is becoming the character of an officer and a gentleman, and that, indifferent to the peace and order of the regiment, he is unmindful of the rules of military discipline. His conduct then becomes the proper subject of inquiry and adjudication before a Court Martial.

In all such cases, however, it must be desirable-to exclude the possibility of misconstruction. And as the new articles point out with clearness the course which is consistent with the character of honourable men, it will be the duty of those who may have to frame charges, as well as of those to whose revision and correction, or approval, charges may be submitted, to take care that the offence be described in language which shall distinctly state those particulars in which the letter or spirit of Her Majesty's Articles of War has been neglected or violated.

I have, &c.

(Signed)   J.NICHOLL

This Letter of Instruction is so well calculated to set at rest any erroneous impressions which may have existed on this point, and places the question of framing charges in reference to the 31st Article of War on a footing so clear and intelligible, that it is only necessary for me to express my entire concurrence in the principles so ably laid down by the Judge Advocate General.

I have, &c.

(Signed)   H. HARDINGE,

Secretary at War.

Appendix C2 – Relevant Articles of War

The Articles of War referred to in the foregoing Observations.

15.-ALL. Officers, of what Condition soever, have Power to quell all Quarrels, Frays, and Disorders, though the Persons concerned should be of superior Rank, or belong to another Corps, and either to order Officers into Arrest, or Soldiers into Confinement, until their proper Superior Officers shall be acquainted therewith.

16.-NO Officer shall use any reproachful or provoking Speeches or Gestures to another, upon Pain of being put in Arrest.

17.-WE hereby declare Our Approbation of the Conduct of all those who, having had the Misfortune of giving Offence to, or of injuring or of insulting others, shall frankly explain, apologize, or offer Redress for the same; or who, having had the Misfortune of receiving Offence, Injury, or Insult from another, shall. cordially accept frank Explanation, Apology, or Redress for the same; or who, if such Explanations, Apology, or Redress are refused to be made or accepted, and the Friends of the Parties shall have failed to adjust the Difference, shall submit the Matter to be dealt with by the Commanding Officer of the Regiment or Detachment, Fort or Garrison; - and We accordingly acquit of Disgrace or Opinion of Disadvantage all Officers who, being willing to make or accept such Redress, refuse to accept Challenges, as they will only have acted as is suitable to the Character of Honourable Men, and have done their Duty as good Soldiers who subject themselves to Discipline.

44.-ANY Officer who, being concerned in any Fray, shall refuse to obey any other Officer, (though of inferior Rank,) who shall order him into Arrest; or shall draw his Sword upon or offer Violence to such Officer, shall, for each and every one of the aforesaid Offences, on Conviction thereof before a General Court-martial, be CASHIERED. -

101.- EVERY Officer who shall give, send, convey, or promote a Challenge, or who shall accept any Challenge to fight a Duel with another Officer, or who shall assist as a Second at a Duel, or who, being privy to an Intention to fight a Duel, shall not take active Measures to prevent such Duel, or who shall upbraid another for refusing or for not giving a Challenge, or who shall reject or advise the Rejection of a reasonable Proposition made for the honourable Adjustment of a Difference, shall be liable, if convicted before a General Court-martial, to be cashiered, or suffer such other Punishment as the Court may award.

IN the event of an Officer being brought to a Court-martial for having assisted as a Second in a Duel, if it shall appear that such Officer had strenuously exerted himself to effect an Adjustment of the Difference on Terms consistent with the Honour of both the Parties, and shall have failed through the Unwillingness of the adverse Parties to accept Terms of honourable Accommodation, then Our Will and Pleasure is that such Officer shall suffer such Punishment, other than cashiering, as the Court may award.

Appendix D
The decision in Perry's first Trial

Horse Guards, 9th August 1854.

The General Commanding-in-Chief having had the honor to lay before Her Majesty the Queen the Proceedings of the General Court Martial holden at Windsor on the 12th July, 1854, and continued by adjournments until the 14th July 1854, for the trial of Lieutenant James Edward Perry of the 46th Regiment, who was arraigned upon the undermentioned charge, viz :

CHARGE -" For conduct unbecoming an officer and a gentleman, and to the prejudice of good order and military discipline, in having, at Windsor on or about the night of the 28th, or morning of the 29th June, 1854, committed an outrageous assault on Lieutenant Thomas Fergus Greer of the 46th Regiment, and grievously wounded the said Lieutenant Greer by beating him on the head and face with a pair of candlesticks."

Upon which charge the Court came to the following decision:-
"The Court having maturely weighed and considered the evidence in support of the prosecution, together with what the prisoner, Lieutenant James Edward Perry, 46th Regiment, has urged in his defence, does now find, and is of opinion, that he the prisoner, Lieutenant James Edward Perry, 46th Regiment, is Guilty of the whole of the charge preferred against him.

"The Court having found the prisoner, Lieutenant James Edward Perry, 46th Regiment guilty of the charge preferred against him, which being in breach of the Articles of War, does now sentence the prisoner, Lieutenant James Edward Perry, 46th Regiment, to be dismissed Her Majesty's Service."

Windsor Barracks, July 14th, 1854

The Judge Advocate General of Her Majesty's Forces.
SIR, I have the honour to acquaint you that I am requested by the unanimous desire of the members of the Court Martial of which I am President, held upon Lieutenant Perry, of the 46th Regiment, to

recommend the prisoner to the favourable consideration of Her Majesty, in consequence of his youth, and the amount of gross provocation he appears to have received from Lieutenant Greer of the same Regiment.

I have, &c., (Signed) James LINDSAY,
Captain and Lieut.-Col and Bt.-Col. Grenadier Guards.President.

It appeared on the Record (page 11) that the Court was cleared for the purpose' of deliberating on the following question put by the prisoner on the cross-examination of Lieutenant T. F. Greer, first witness:

" Did you not seize me by the breast and throat, and throw me on my bed; and did I not order you under arrest, which you refused to obey, saying you would see me damned first?"

The Court was re-opened, and decided that the question should not be put to the evidence.

The Deputy Judge Advocate General, in the absence of the Judge Advocate General, being, of opinion that the prisoner had been thereby precluded from putting a question to the witness which was legally admissible and relevant to the issue, humbly submitted that Her Majesty should be pleased not to confirm the proceedings.

For the above reasons, communicated from the Judge Advocate General's Office on the 7th, instant, Her Majesty was graciously pleased not to confirm the proceedings of the Court.

By direction of the General Commanding-in-Chief,

C. YORKE, *Military Secretary*

Appendix E - The decision in Greer's Trial

GENERAL ORDER No.542.

Horse Guards, 2nd September 1854.

At a General Court Martial held at Windsor, on the 21st July, 1854, Lieutenant Thomas Fergus Greer, of the 46th Regiment, was arraigned. upon the under-mentioned charge, viz.:-

" For conduct unbecoming an officer and a gentleman, and to the prejudice of good order and military discipline, in the following instances: -

First,- In having, at Windsor, on or about the night of the 28th or the morning of the 29th June 1854, wilfully struck and offered other personal violence to Lieutenant James Edward Perry, of the 46th Regiment,

Second, - In having at the time and place last above mentioned used provoking, insulting, and disgusting language towards the said Lieutenant Perry, by calling him 'swindler;' 'blackguard,' and by using other expressions towards him of a most offensive and insulting nature."

Upon which charge the Court came to the following decision: --

"The Court having maturely weighed and considered the whole of the evidence before it, together with what the prisoner, has urged in his defence, are of opinion that he, the prisoner, Lieutenant Thomas Fergus Greer, of the 46th Regiment, is *not Guilty* of that part of the charge contained in the first instance of, it, viz. –In having at Windsor, on or about the night of, the 28th,or morning of the 29th June 1854, wilfully, struck and offered other personal violence to Lieutenant James Edward. Perry, of the 46th Regiment, and do therefore acquit' him of the same; and the Court are of opinion that he, the prisoner, Lieutenant Thomas Fergus Greer, of the 46th Regiment, is guilty of the whole of that part of the charge contained in the second instance of it, viz. :-In having at the time and place last above mentioned used provoking, insulting, and disgusting language towards the said Lieutenant Perry, by calling him 'swindler,' 'blackguard,' and by using other expressions towards him of a most offensive and insulting nature; with the exception of using the precise words, 'swindler,' 'blackguard,' of which they acquit him.

The Court having found the prisoner *Guilty* of a part of the charge preferred against him as above specified, which, being in breach of the Articles of War, do now by virtue thereof adjudge him, the prisoner, Lieutenant Thomas Fergus Greer, of the 46th Regiment, to be severely reprimanded, and further to be reduced on the list of Lieutenants of the 46th Regiment, and to be placed next below Lieutenant Nicholas Dunscombe, of the 46th Regiment."

It appeared on the record that two witnesses were examined on the part of the prosecution:-

First, Lieutenant James Edward Perry; Second, Esther Major. - The first witness gave positive and detailed evidence of several distinct acts of personal violence committed against him by the prisoner on the occasion in question ; and the record discloses no ground for deeming the testimony of this witness, as given in chief, to have been rendered less worthy of credit by cross-examination. The evidence of the second witness, although it does not directly confirm that of the first, as to particular details of personal violence, on the' one hand does not contradict it, and on the other seems indirectly to corroborate it by agreeing with it in many particulars, the reality of which there seems no reason to doubt, and which, if they actually occurred, would render it probable that acts of personal violence were really committed by the prisoner, and that he made use of the expressions specified in the second instance of the charge.

The evidence adduced. by the prisoner cannot reasonably be regarded either as contradicting the testimony of the first witness in any particular materially affecting the issues to be tried, or as showing that the witness was wholly unworthy of credit.

Nor can the address of the prisoner reasonably be considered to have impaired the value or altered the effect of the evidence for the prosecution.

It thus appearing that the finding of the Court, on the first instance of the charge, was without warrant, as being against, evidence, and that so much of the finding of the Court in the second instance as is comprised in the words '~ with the exception of using the precise words ` swindler,' ' blackguard,' of which they acquit him,' was also without warrant; as being against evidence ;" .

The Deputy Judge Advocate: General, in the absence of the Judge Advocate-General, humbly submitted that Her Majesty should be graciously pleased to order the Court to be re-assembled, with a view to a revision of the proceedings on the grounds above set forth.

For the above reason Her Majesty was graciously pleased to order the Court to be re-assembled, with a view to a revision of the proceedings.

Horse Guards, 11th August 1854.

The General Court Martial having this day re-assembled in compliance with the orders of the General Commanding-in-Chief, signifying Her Majesty's commands, that the former sentence shall be revised by the Court, and stating the grounds on which such commands have been given by Her Majesty; which documents were laid before the Court by the Deputy Judge Advocate, together with the original proceedings of the Court held for the trial of Lieutenant Thomas Fergus Greer, of the 46th Regiment; "The Court, having carefully re-considered the evidence that was brought before them during the trial, beg most respectfully to adhere to their former decision."

Her Majesty was pleased not to confirm and approve the finding and sentence of the Court.

The General Commanding-in-Chief felt it his duty humbly to submit to Her Majesty the sense he entertained of

223

Lieutenant Greer's conduct throughout these transactions.

As a witness before the first Court Martial which tried Lieutenant Perry, he repeatedly declined to answer the questions put to him by the prisoner, Lieutenant Perry, which were necessary for the discovery of the truth, on the plea that he would thereby criminate himself.

When on his own trial, it is clearly established by evidence then taken, that Lieutenant Greer had applied the most disgusting expressions to Lieutenant Perry.

The evidence on the preceding trial of Lieutenant Perry is also confirmatory of these facts, and ˉthey admit of no reasonable doubt.

Such ungentlemanlike conduct is calculated to degrade an officer in the eyes of his men, and to destroy his power of maintaining discipline.

A person who does not shrink from the utterance of such disgraceful language is unfit to preserve his position of social equality in a regiment amongst his brother officers.

He cannot exchange into another regiment, for the officers would refuse to receive him; and they would be entitled so to do under Her Majesty's regulations.

The General Commanding-in-Chief could not omit to mark with the expression of the severest displeasure the gambling propensities of Lieutenant Greer.

But, without reference to these propensities, the misconduct, already adverted to is fully sufficient to call for his removal from the Army.

On these grounds, the General Commanding-in-Chief humbly submitted to Her Majesty, that Lieutenant Greer should be removed from the service by the sale of his commission, which recommendation Her Majesty has been graciously pleased to sanction.

By Command of   The General Commanding-in-Chief,

C. YORKE, *Military Secretary*

Appendix F: The decision in Perry's Second Trial

GENERAL ORDER No. 543.

Horse Guards, 2nd September 1854.

At a General Court Martial holden at Windsor on the 28th day of July 1854, and continued by adjournments to the 21st August 1854, Lieutenant. James Edward Perry, of the 46th Regiment, was arraigned upon the undermentioned charge, viz:-

For scandalous, infamous conduct, unbecoming an Officer and a Gentleman, in the following instances:-

First-"For having in a certain letter, dated Windsor Barracks, July 24th, 1854, and addressed to Colonel The Honourable Arthur Upton, President of the Court Martial then and there assembled for, the Trial of Lieutenant T. F. Greer, which letter bore the signature of the prisoner; and was then and there delivered to the said Colonel Upton -- made the following slanderous statement respecting his commanding officer, Lieutenant Colonel. Garrett, viz. :-'that after repeated acts of violence against myself (meaning the prisoner) (by other officers of the 46th while, the regiment was in Dublin) in my Bedroom, I reported the circumstances to Colonel Garrett, who reproached me, and called me a fool for my pains;' he the said prisoner then well knowing that so much of the said statement as relates to Lieutenant Colonel Garrett, viz. : the words `who reproached me and called me a fool for my pains,' was false."

Second-" For having in the said letter made the following statement: 'I then patiently submitted to a series of indignities, when I complained to Major Maxwell, who represented the facts to Colonel. Garrett, upon which he gave the offenders a reprimand ; so weak was the effect of the reprimand or caution given by Colonel Garrett, that though the acts of aggression

225

were discontinued, I was persecuted in other ways, until I threatened to appeal to the General of the district, and sent a letter to that effect to Colonel Garrett. On it being known that I was determined upon such a course, I was earnestly entreated, by several of my brother officers, to forbear making any complaint. I did forbear, and from that time I was relieved from any repetition of the annoyances and indignities under which I had formerly laboured,-he, the prisoner, then " well knowing that so much of the said statement with reference to Colonel Garrett, as is comprised in the following words, -- 'Until I threatened to appeal to the General of the district, and sent a letter to that effect to Colonel Garrett,' --was false,-- and that he, the prisoner, had never made any threat to Colonel Garrett, either by word of mouth or in writing, that he would appeal to the General of the district.

Third-" For having, on the 21st day of July 1854, at Windsor, when examined as a witness before the Court Martial, which was then and there being held for the trial of Lieutenant Thomas Fergus Greer, in reply to the following question: ' Will you swear positively that Captain Nicholas did not reprimand officers against whom you had made a complaint to the commanding officer,-made the following answer: 'I have taken an oath already, Captain Nicholas never, to my knowledge, censured anybody; he himself (meaning Captain Nicholas), having ill-treated others on joining,' -he, the prisoner then well knowing that so much of the said answer, as is comprised in the following words, he himself having ill-treated others on joining' --was false."

The Court having found the prisoner *Guilty* of the Second, Third, and Fourth Instances of the Charge preferred against him, and performed the painful duty of sentencing him to be *Cashiered* in strict conformity to the Articles of War, which deprived them of all discretionary power, taking into its consideration the youth and inexperience of the prisoner -- the exciting and painful position he stood in at the time the letters were written on which the charge is founded, -- and the circumstances disclosed in evidence' under which they were signed by him, begs leave humbly to recommend the prisoner to Her Majesty's clemency on the grounds of his having acted under illjudged counsel and influence, in committing so grave a breach of military order and discipline.

Her Majesty has been pleased to approve and confirm the finding and sentence of the Court.

The Deputy Judge Advocate-General having submitted to Her Majesty the proceedings, in the case of Lieutenant Perry, and Her Majesty having been advised to approve and confirm the finding and sentence of the Court in all that regards the legal points relating to the Judge Advocate-General's Department; the General Commanding-in-Chief humbly submitted to Her Majesty that the finding and sentence be approved on military grounds.

The importance of upholding discipline and good order in Her Majesty's service imposed upon the General Commanding-in-Chief the necessity of submitting to Her Majesty, that the sentence passed by the Court on the prisoner should be carried into effect, notwithstanding the recommendation of the Court in his favour, and the reason assigned for that recommendation.

No commanding officer would be safe in the discharge of his duties if inferior officers could with impunity make accusations similar to those of which Lieutenant Perry has been found guilty.

The prisoner has been acquitted on the first instance of the charge, but found guilty of the second, third, and fourth instances, and has been sentenced to be cashiered.

227

When an officer has been found guilty of such charges, and sentenced to be cashiered, and that the legality of the proceedings of the Court awarding such a Sentence has been confirmed by the two departments whose duty it is to submit to Her Majesty their opinions, the General Commanding-in-Chief has only one means of giving effect to the Court's recommendation for Her Majesty's clemency, which was, to solicit Her Majesty to permit the prisoner to receive the amount of his commissions; and this recommendation Her Majesty has been graciously pleased to approve.

Lieutenant Perry was appointed to an Ensigncy in January 1853, without purchase, solely on account of his father's very meritorious services in the Army; he subsequently purchased his Lieutenantcy.

The General Commanding-in-Chief cannot close his observations on these proceedings without noticing the letter of Lieutenant William Waldy.

The letter of Lieutenant William Waldy, addressed to Lieutenant Perry, on the 2nd June 1854, is not to be reconciled with his evidence' given before the Court Martial which tried Lieutenant Perry a few weeks afterwards.

In the letter he states that Captain Nicholas ˉhad applied a very insulting epithet to Ensign Coote at the mess table, and that the latter had given the lie direct to Captain Nicholas.

As a witness on oath, before the Court Martial, he denies or forgets that he had written such a letter; even if he did forget, his levity is deserving the severest reprehension.

After the Court had closed its proceedings, Lieutenant

William Waldy was called upon by his commanding officer to explain his conduct in this matter.

He stated in his explanation, that he must have given a higher colour to the affair than it merited that since the affair scarce an officer has. spoken to him -and that in a foolish moment he wrote the strong language recorded against him in his letter. Lieutenant William Waldy appears to be a weak gossiping young man, insensible of the duty of a rigid adherence to the truth in describing the conduct of others; and incapable of estimating the mischievous consequences of exaggerating a contradiction at the mess table into the lie direct, by which departure from the truth the character of his brother officers might have been seriously affected.

He does not appear, however, to have been actuated by any malicious motives, and, in the absence of any proof of corrupt intention, the General Commanding-in-Chief hereby directs, with Her Majesty's sanction, that Lieutenant William Waldy be severely reprimanded, and cautioned, for the rest of his life, to adhere strictly to the truth.

      By Command of
         The General Commanding-in-Chief,
            C. YORKE,   *Military Secretary*

THE WINDSOR COURTS-MARTIAL

Appendix G – Hart's Army List 1854: 46th Foot

46th (*The South Devonshire*) *Regt. of Foot.*   197

"DOMINICA."

Years' Serv.		
56		**Colonel.**
		ꝑ ꝗꝉ Richard Egerton,[1] *CB. Ens.* 1 Dec. 98; *Lt.* 29 March, 00; *Capt.* 28
Full Pay.	Half Pay.	Sept. 04; *Major*, 26 Aug. 13; *Lieut.-Col.* 18 June 15; *Col.* 10 Jan. 37; *Major-Gen.* 9 Nov. 46; *Col.* 46th Foot, 24 Jan. 53.
28	14⅚	**Lieutenant-Colonel.**
		ꝑ Robert Garrett,[2] *KH. Ens.* ꝑ 6 March, 11; *Lt.* 3 Sept. 12; *Capt.* ꝑ 7 July, 14 , *Major*, ꝑ 19 Sept. 26; *Brevet-Lt.-Col.* 23 Nov. 41; *Lt.-Col.* ꝑ 16 May 45.
		Majors.
19	0	Alexander Maxwell, *Ens.* ꝑ 19 June 35; *Lieut.* ꝑ 28 Dec. 38; *Capt.* ꝑ 27 Sept. 42; *Major*, ꝑ 19 Sept. 48.
18	0	David Fyffe, *Ens.* ꝑ 11 June 36; *Lieut.* 2 Apr. 41; *Capt.* ꝑ 16 May 45; *Major*, ꝑ 16 Dec. 53.

Years		CAPTAINS.	ENSIGN.	LIEUT.	CAPTAIN.	BREV.-MAJ.
19	0	Arthur George Vesey ..	ꝑ 29 May 35	ꝑ 25 Aug. 37	ꝑ 22 July 42	
15	0	Arthur Wombwell, *s.* ..	ꝑ 5 Apr. 39	ꝑ 29 Oct. 41	ꝑ 8 May 46	
20	0	William Henry O'Toole	ꝑ 12 Dec. 34	31 May 39	8 Jan. 47	
14	0	Colin Fred. Campbell ..	1 May 40	10 Mar. 42	ꝑ 13 Aug. 47	
13	0	Algernon Robert Garrett	1 June 41	ꝑ 27 Sept. 42	ꝑ 28 Apr. 48	
12	0	George Caldwell Dickens	ꝑ 27 May 42	21 Apr. 46	ꝑ 11 Apr. 51	
12	0	Horace George Hayes ..	ꝑ 24 June 42	ꝑ 25 Nov. 45	ꝑ 9 May 51	
12	0	Robert William Piper ..	28 May 42	ꝑ 11 July 45	ꝑ 23 Apr. 52	
12	0	William Hardy	ꝑ 27 Sept. 42	ꝑ 8 May 46	12 Oct. 52	
11	0	John Edward Lyons	ꝑ 3 Mar. 43	ꝑ 6 Nov. 46	ꝑ 16 Dec. 53	
		LIEUTENANTS.				
13	0	Henry Fuller Sandwith, *adj.*	ꝑ 30 Oct. 41	26 Apr. 44		
12	0	Chas. Robert Shervinton	20 May 42	6 July 45		
10	0	James George Clarke ..	26 Apr. 44	22 Feb. 47		
10	0	John H. Chambers	31 May 44	30 Mar. 47		
10	0	Albert Nicholas	ꝑ 6 Dec. 44	ꝑ 13 Aug. 47		
9	0	George Fred. Dallas ...	ꝑ 16 May 45	ꝑ 28 Apr. 48		
8	0	Cha. Somerville McAlester	ꝑ 6 Nov. 46	ꝑ 10 Nov. 48		
6	0	William Reginald Hesketh	ꝑ 21 July 48	ꝑ 23 Apr. 52		
5	0	Thomas Fergus Greer ..	ꝑ 29 May 49	ꝑ 12 Oct. 52		
5	0	John Augustus Fane	ꝑ 19 Oct. 49	31 Dec. 52		
5	0	Alfred Henry Waldy	ꝑ 14 Dec. 49	ꝑ 1 Apr. 53		
5	0	Richard Lluellyn	15 Dec. 49	ꝑ 28 Oct. 53		
		ENSIGNS.				
4	0	Frank John Curtis......	ꝑ 22 Nov. 50			
2	0	Thomas Douglas Forde..	ꝑ 15 Oct. 52			
2	0	Nicholas Dunscombe....	ꝑ 23 Nov. 52			
1	0	James Edward Perry ..	18 Feb. 53			
1	0	George Henry Knapp ..	ꝑ 11 Mar. 53			
1	0	William Thomas Waldy ..	ꝑ 22 Apr. 53			
1	0	George Morland Hutton	ꝑ 28 Oct. 53			
1	0	Richard Coote	ꝑ 11 Nov. 53			
1	0	Geo. D. Thos. Stockwell	ꝑ 16 Dec. 53			

2 Lieut.-Col. Garrett served in the Peninsula with the 6th Division in 1811, and with the 4th Division in 1812 and 13, and was present in all the actions, sieges, and smaller affairs in which those two Divisions were respectively engaged from Fuentes d'Onor in May 1811, until the end of 1813, when he was sent to England for recovery from his wounds. He received two wounds at the attack of the Forts at Salamanca, on which occasion the command of the Light Company of the Queen's and some Artillery devolved upon him, he being the only surviving officer of the column he attacked with; and he was again severely wounded in the Pyrenees. He has received the War Medal with four clasps for Fuentes d'Onor, Salamanca, Vittoria, and Pyrenees.

6 Paymaster Corcoran served the Coorg campaign in the East Indies with the 48th, in 1834.
7 Qr.-Master Scoltock served with the 46th at the siege and capture of Kittoor in Dec. 1824.

16	0	*Paymaster.*—Alexis Corcoran,[5] 8 July 42; *Ens.* 30 Nov. 38; *Lt.* 8 April 42.
13	0	*Adjutant.*—*Lieut.* Henry Fuller Sandwith, 16 Jan. 52.
8	0	*Quarter-Master.*—Samuel Scoltock,[7] 13 March 46.
28	0	*Surgeon.*—Wm. Irwin Breslin, M.D. 2 July, 41; *Assist.-Surg.* 8 March, 27 ; *Hosp.-Assist.* 9 Feb. 26.
5	0	*Assistant-Surgeon.*—Edward James Franklyn, 19 Oct. 49.

Facings Yellow.

Agents, Messrs. Cox & Co.— *Irish Agents*, Sir E. R. Borough, *Bt.*, Armit, & Co.
[*Returned from North America*, 8 May 1848.]

Select Bibliography

Contemporary sources

Various General Orders and letters from Horse Guards ordered to be read to all officers and in particular the letter dated 2 September 1854; General Orders 542 and 543.

The National Archives: WO3/498; WO3/499; WO3/566; WO81/99; WO82/14; WO85/8; WO92/2; WO93/13; WO93/15;

Parliamentary Papers, 1857-8 Vol XXXVII *(Return of Officers tried by GCM)*

Parliamentary Papers, 1857-8 Vol XXXVIII *(the Medical History of regiments in Crimea).*

The Times: reports almost daily during the three trials, innumerable leading articles and many readers' letters, from 14 July 1854 to 23 December 1854.

Colburn's United Services Journal

United Service Magazine

Punch, or the London Charivari

The Bedford Times

Annual Register 1854

Books

Corelli Barnett, *Britain and her Army,* pub 1970.

CC Bayley, *Mercenaries for the Crimea,* pub Montreal 1977,

Sir William Blackstone, *Commentaries on the Laws of England,* many editions, Oxford.

Frederick Campbell, *Letters from Sevastopol, 1854-5,* pub Bentley, London, 1894.

Philip D. Curtin, *Death by Migration,* Cambridge University Press, 1989.

D'Aguilar, Major –General, *Observations on the practice and forms of District, Regimental and Detachment Courts Martial,* pub Dublin, 1850.

Alan J Guy, *Oeconomy and Discipline,* pub 1985.

Hart's Army List, 1854, 55, and 60.

Elizabeth Longford, *Wellington, Pillar of State,* pub London 1972.
Michael Hargreave Mawson, *Eye Witness in the Crimea,* pub London, Greenhill (Frederick Dallas' papers)
Frederick Myatt, *The British Infantry 1660-1945.*
Victor Neuberg, *Gone for a Soldier,* pub London 1989.
Queen's Regulations and Orders for the Army 1844.
Major Colin Robins, *The Murder of a Regiment,* pub Bowdon, 1994. (Lt Llewellyn's journal)
Major Colin Robins, *Captain Dunscombe's Diary: the real Crimean War,* pub Bowdon, 2003
TF Simmons, *Simmons on Court-Martials,*4th Edition, 1852.
EM Spiers, *The Army and Society, 1815-1914.*
John Strawson, *Beggars in Red*
Myra Trustram, *Women of the Regiment, Marriage and the Victorian Army,* pub Cambridge, 1984.
E.S.Turner, *Gallant Gentlemen,a portrait of the British Officer, 1600-1956,* pub London, 1956.
William Waldy, *From Eight to Eighty,* pub London, Harrison.
Noel St John Williams, *Judy O'Grady and the Colonel's Lady* (quoting *The Times* for 25 Feb 1854.)

Articles
(JSAHR = Journal of the Society for Army Historical Research)
Lt Col H Moyse-Bartlett in 'The British army in 1850', *JSAHR,* Vol 52, (1954)
Hew Strachan,'The early Victorian army and the nineteenth-century revolution in government', *The English Historical Review,* Vol 95 (1980).
CB Otley, 'The Social Origins of British Army Officers', in *The Sociological Review,* Vol 18, no 2 (1970).
FstC Vivian's article 'John André as a Young Officer', *JSAHR,* Vol 40, (1962)